The Business of
Architectural Practice

The Business of
Architectural Practice

Derek Sharp
DipArch(Hons), FRIBA, FBIM, FCIArb

COLLINS
8 Grafton Street, London W1

Collins Professional and Technical Books
William Collins Sons & Co. Ltd
8 Grafton Street, London W1X 3LA

First published in Great Britain by
Collins Professional and Technical Books 1986

Distributed in the United States of America
by Sheridan House, Inc.

Copyright © Derek Sharp 1986

British Library Cataloguing in Publication Data
Sharp, Derek
The business of architectural practice.
1. Architectural practice — Great Britain
— Management
I. Title
720'.68   NA1996

ISBN 0-00-383182-5

Typeset by Columns of Reading
Printed and bound in Great Britain by
Mackays of Chatham, Kent

Contents

Acknowledgements to

My wife, Vera — For statistical information – and for being patient

My secretary, Ann Hayden — For organisation and reams of typing

Terry Dacombe — For information on decennial insurance

Alan Bonner — For graphics

My accountant, Geoff Heatherington — For accountancy advice

My insurance broker, Tatton Brown — For insurance advice

Derek Tatnall — For general advice

Introduction

Some years ago, when I used to prepare building management case studies for teaching, I would send copies of these studies to the Harvard Graduate Business School. In return they sent me case studies of building problems they were using on their course. One day I received a telephone call from Tom Raymond, Dean of Administration at Harvard Graduate Business School, who was over in England and wanted to meet me. We agreed a time and date and he said he would come to my office and then go for lunch. On the appointed day he arrived early and was brought into my room by my secretary. He was a man of medium height, a plump and cheerful American, who shook me by the hand, gripped my elbow and said: 'Pleased to meet you, Derek.' (First names already!!)

He sat down in front of my desk, put both elbows on the desk, hands under his chin, and said with his face about a foot away from mine: 'Well Derek, what's your business?'

I retreated to the back of my chair, paused and replied: 'What do you mean, what's my business?' He said: 'I mean, what business are you in?'. I said: 'I am an architect'.

He smiled, spread his hands and said: 'You're in the architects' business then'. I answered hesitantly: 'Well, yes'. 'What is an architect's business?' he asked. I thought for a moment and said 'Well, we're professionals, we provide services to our clients and design buildings.'

'So, you're in the building design business,' he said. 'Not exactly, there's more to it than that,' I countered. 'Well, what business are you in then?' he demanded. 'What do you actually do? I suppose you don't actually build the buildings?' 'No,' I said. 'So, what do you do?' I said: 'Well, we take instructions from our clients, design the building, get their approval and produce information for builders and quantity surveyors, then see that the builder builds in accordance with the information.'

Tom Raymond took his elbows off the desk, looked at me and said: 'Well, Derek, I guess you're in the building design information and supervision business.' I looked at him, thinking, 'I suppose he's really right', that's what architects do in Great Britain. 'So,' he said, 'do you manage it well, Derek?'. I replied rather humbly: 'I try to'. This book is about trying to manage our architectural businesses well.

Some architects regard their practice purely as a design organisation, the prime consideration being the quality of the final design. Others regard their main objective as being buildings of quality, which they have guided through to completion. For others their main objective is seen as the provision of professional services of varying kinds to satisfy clients associated with the building industry. Others, more financially orientated, regard the bottom line as being pounds profit per annum.

The objectives of architects should in fact be a combination of all these points, quality buildings, optimum professional services with benefits and profits, for their clients and themselves.

1 Architecture is a business

The architect carries the authority, responsibility and account-ability for the work which is placed with him by his clients. The client gives the architect the power to carry out specific tasks and be accountable for the actions taken. The client relies on the architect's experience, judgment and integrity in the discharge of this work, for which he is paid a fee. This fee must cover all his costs and there must be a surplus.

The architect who takes on this responsibility is running an architectural business.

THE ARCHITECT'S POWER TO PERFORM SERVICES

The architect has no power to act without the authority of the client unless he takes over the authority himself and pays for the cost of the work involved. This may be necessary in a case where an architect wants to obtain sufficient information regarding a site in order to offer it to a client and take the risk of the proposal being refused and hence being aborted at his own cost.

The architect in business has to accept and be able to perform different categories of responsibility. They are as follows.

Advisory

This relates to the consultancy work which goes on before a project is commenced where the client requires advice on various aspects related to the possibilities of a building being com-missioned. Advice is also sought throughout the various stages of the building process on the various aspects of the architect's work and also often about the proposals of other consultants and professional advisers.

I have found that once you establish a trusting relationship with clients your advice is sought on many other decisions which they — and sometimes even their families — are seeking to take. I can remember helping to choose a new Rolls Royce and dresses for weddings, meeting the fiancés of clients' daughters, being asked to find out the background of potential spouses, being best man at weddings and acting as intermediary in complicated family wedding arrangements, and many other intriguing extra-professional advisory duties.

The normal architectural service

This relates to preliminary, basic and other services which are offered and are described in the Architect's Appointment published by the Royal Institute of British Architects (RIBA).

I have for many years advised my architectural students to do what I do at least once a year, that is to read through the Architect's Appointment. I always find that I have overlooked something vital to one of my current projects, and next day hastily try to make amends. The main omission seems to relate to extra services for which I have not charged and to which we are rightfully entitled. Sometimes I find that either the client or I have actually changed the nature of a commission but that I have omitted to point out the consequences in fee percentages or the scope of the work to the client.

Today there are so many variations from the 'normal' service that it may soon be necessary to have an extension catalogue of services on offer to make clear to clients the exact nature of the architect's engagement.

Legal

An architect is expected to have a working knowledge of the law of property, statutory controls related to buildings and building contracts.

If you are a good communicator and have a good general knowledge of the law, as most architects who act as arbitrators have, it is nonetheless vital that you do not allow yourself to be regarded as an expert in legal matters. I have found clients phoning me about their legal problems because sometimes they are perplexed by the social and moral implications of decisions which they have obtained from their lawyers in purely legal terms.

Any advice an architect gives should be covered by a disclaimer of any authority or expertise and it should be emphasised that the advice is only given in an effort to help the client think through a legal problem. Don't get drawn into disputes, particularly between partners. You are bound to lose one or possibly both clients.

Setting up a business

This involves providing staff and resources for the services which are to be performed by the office, to ensure that projects are efficiently run and co-ordinated with the other members of the building team.

Most people view architects as running a business concerned with building. They usually have the idea that we sit at drawing boards all day dispensing drawn information. The fact is that most senior architects spend the majority of their time behind a desk, directing their business, communicating with clients and dealing with strategic aspects of project management.

Overseeing and inspecting

This aspect of an architect's job is to ensure that the work done in design and construction is in accordance with the requirements of the client, and with good practice in the building industry. When operations start on site he must see that the information is properly interpreted and executed correctly.

There is a growing body of opinion that architects should withdraw from supervision work because of the harsh penalties the courts have laid down in cases of negligence. In such cases there is now a tendency to sue everyone in sight, and some of the most vulnerable are architects. An architect should always impress on a client the realities of site inspection and what can reasonably be expected from building professionals and consultants.

Interests of society

In order to maintain his client's best interests, it is the duty of the architect to remind the client of the present and long term interests of society as a whole in relation to what the client has instructed him to do.

Personal, political and social inclinations often colour the attitude of the architect in relation to his client's instructions and intentions. Over-zealous protection of society or interested groups can alienate clients or sometimes have the opposite effect of drawing client and architect together in a cause for public good.

A dispassionate independent professional view has always been my approach to this ever changing aspect of professional practice.

Willingness to perform

The architect must have a dedication to the performance of his work and a willingness to use all his skills for the benefit of his clients. He must ensure through delegation that all others involved in the building project share this attitude towards optimum performance on their clients' behalf.

Motivation, enthusiasm, determination, tenacity, energy and drive must come together for the benefit of the client. Demands are made upon the stamina of the architect and a healthy and balanced lifestyle is necessary to cope with these demands.

Judgment of performance

The architect must be accountable for the performance of the business, and be sure that the client gets what he really needs, with a building provided on time, at the right cost and of the quality required.

The architect must therefore be accountable for the overall performance of the project, and must be able to show where accountability lies in areas outside his responsibility. The individuals in the office must also be accountable for the profitability of the project and the maintenance of an effective leadership and happy team of people working together on a successful operation. Architects accepting the authority, responsibility and accountability for the jobs and running their offices as efficient undertakings will therefore expect to run a rewarding business which is satisfying and fulfilling to all those who take part.

Sometimes, despite the best management, architects face losses, are sued, become exhausted and give up the battle for survival in practice. In all businesses we hear about the extremes of success and failure but little about the great majority who keep producing a service to a high standard of competence. It is to these practices that this book is dedicated in the hope that it will help them to run a better practice.

MANAGING THE BUSINESS

Objectives

Architecture as a business entails running an office as a profitable undertaking and, inside that office, running individual jobs efficiently. Architecture, like all businesses, has some underlying principles which require positive action. It is important to define in clear terms the purpose and objectives of the office, the type of services it will offer, and the rewards it expects to achieve. It is not always easy to define objectives because, unless the leadership is absolutely clear in its goals, different members of the hierarchy may have varying views on the aims of the office. It is up to those in charge to see that the specific goals of the business are clearly communicated to all those who participate in it.

I remember advising a practice in the north of Britain regarding a merger with another local practice. One practice was based solely on local authority work while the other was a commercial practice. They thought that in combining the two areas of work, they could cover a greater part of the market and in times of cut backs, if one area of business was in recession, the other could tide them over. It sounded like common sense and the merger occurred. Within three years the practice had been shattered by divisions between the old partners and the new. The new partners, who had accepted the amalgamation, were trying to make it work well only to be frustrated by the old partners who could never accept change of objective.

Eventually the practice split up, one partner retired, the commercial senior partner took over, others set up the old local authority based practice again and one went abroad.

Architectural practice, like all businesses, relies on the attitudes which underlie the emotional energy of the principals. In any partnership it is the duty of all to keep the objectivity and emotional 'chemistry' in balance and to believe in unity of purpose.

The nature of the professional office

The structure of the office is the key to success. In my experience not enough time and energy is put into this aspect of our professional lives. The key word for office structure is 'delegation'. Work and staff are divided and unified by leadership into a complex working system, where power, responsibility for the job and an appraisal system can function well. The whole office must be kept in a state of equilibrium from day to day, despite the erratic external changes which affect us at all times.

Running a professional office is really rather different from running other businesses. It is generally very important to architects that the office environment is of a particular nature which will enable people to work creatively and well within its confines. Along with the environmental factors there must be an organisational structure which is the framework of all the authority, responsibility and accountability of those who partici-pate in the activities of the office.

Importance of a structure

A clearly defined structure is an essential part of an architect's office and requires constant appraisal to ensure its flexibility and applicability to the needs of the people within the office. These needs change from time to time in relation to external events, and the structure must be reviewed in any period of change, in order to remain sensitive both to external forces and internal requirements. Within the office the work must be under control. We all know how work fluctuates in content particularly as we move through the various processes of a building programme.

Business procedures as a continuing function

It is a prime need of the business to have forecasting, planning, organising, monitoring, co-ordinating and controlling of the project as a continuing operation, reviewed generally on a weekly or at the most a monthly basis.

Forecasting is necessary for projecting targets for budgets, cash flows, project programmes and the costs and time for any special activities.

Planning enables the forecasts to be achieved, sets the necessary yardsticks, objectives and methods for doing the work, and enables the situation to remain flexible so that there is room for change.

Organising provides resources to do the job, in terms of materials, people, plant or whatever is necessary for marshalling the power to get the job moving forward.

Motivating and co-ordinating means getting together staff who are willing to work at the tasks allocated and to proceed harmoniously throughout the programme to completion.

Controlling is the measurement of progress by comparing performance against planned yardsticks in order to monitor progress and show where action is needed by applying the exception principle. This means that what is tolerable as progress is maintained and anything outside that limit is treated as exceptional and acted upon immediately.

Decision making and communication are the activities that bind together these stages of work and make the whole process meaningful.

The same type of management process should be going on for the operation of the office and its financial affairs, ensuring the avoidance of crises and conflict within the office. In order to achieve the smooth running of these procedures it is essential to have an efficient administration which ensures that the objectives of the office are being accurately recorded and compared with the objectives set by the direction. All these activities, which ensure that the business is being properly run, require different types of direction according to the size of the office. They follow the same principles in all practices. The effort which goes into the management of the office increases with the size of the practice.

The present competitive and demanding climate for practice, with tax changes annually which can alter the stability of your structure, the increase in fee competition and the growing tendency of clients to resort to litigation, demands a business-like approach by all architects in order to survive.

2 Getting work and keeping clients

I remember when I was a student being summoned to a special lecture by a leading figure from the RIBA who was to talk to us about professional ethics. At the end of a boring lecture one of the students asked how architects get work. The question evoked a deep red flush to the lecturer's neck and forehead and he refused to answer the question.

There are still many practitioners who feel very uneasy about how they seek work and try to avoid any discussion of the subject. As a result, those who do talk about getting and keeping clients are regarded as being tactless and brash.

In this sort of climate it has been extremely difficult to talk frankly about the subject to students and others. Now, however, with the relaxation of the code of practice and the advent of overseas marketing experts running courses and workshops for architects, this important aspect of an architect's work has at last come into the light.

WHY WE NEED CONTINUALLY TO SEEK WORK

Architects are in a volatile business, and they therefore need to continually seek work. Clients regard their architects as artists, technicians, businessmen and managers, and expect high performance over a wide span of personal abilities. No architect can achieve the ideal of perfection and because we all fail in various ways, clients will not always turn to the same architect, however good his performance. Moreover, as people come and go in large companies, they bring in their own favourite architects so that, however good your performance, you may well be overlooked.

In order to expand the practice you need to be continually

looking for new clients, expanding your expertise, and letting people know what you are doing. Nobody can sit back and assume they have a client for the whole of their professional life.

In the past architects normally got their first jobs from members of their family or friends, new clients often being recommended by satisfied clients or by personal contacts. But these individual clients are now becoming rare and instead we have to seek work from corporate bodies and those who appoint architects are not necessarily at the highest level, but it is they who have to be identified, and they at whom the selling operation must be directed.

In the past there have been ethical problems related to this activity but the professional bodies have now abandoned restrictive codes, allowing advertising, and permitting open competition for everything that the client requires. With the advent of greater competition in a falling market, getting work has become an essential challenge to the architectural practice.

WHERE WORK CAN BE FOUND

Architects have to keep up with the times. They must read newspapers, journals and trade magazines, as well as monitoring radio and television, for construction industry news, opinions and forecasts.

If your business is mainly concerned with government work, part of everyday information gathering will consist in keeping in touch with government policy, including the allocation of money to various departments, and establishing which categories of buildings will be erected with this money.

In the private sector, there are many journals which show trends and areas of business growth which are relevant to architecture. In the field of property development it is often important to know the locations for which developers are searching so that you can find sites and offer them to the developers.

It is useful too, to meet people at social gatherings, listening to what is said and getting leads on who is active in special markets at a certain time, who has money to spend, who is expanding, who is contracting. A firm which is contracting may have properties they wish to sell and this could help your clients.

Often important information can come from your fellow professionals who are likewise seeking work.

Work is therefore found by using the media, through personal contacts, by pursuing hunches, and by scientifically listing targets or seeking sites for clients.

WHO PLACES WORK

Who gives work to architects is a question which most of us ask. Those people who give work to architects are a very small proportion of the total population and are therefore a very select group who have personal or other peoples' money to spend on building.

Clients spending their own money

In the traditional situation where clients are spending their own money, a client will often choose an architect on the basis of recommendation, although some will ask the professional institute for a list of names they can contact when they have a project in mind. In this instance, the person requiring the building, and who is going to occupy it, is the person who must be contacted by the architect. The relationship with this person will be continuous throughout the project and well after occupation. However the individual client is becoming a rarity.

The private company client

The private company may have been set up originally by an extended family, where most of the decisions are made over tea on Sunday afternoon. They will expect you to be by the telephone on Monday morning to receive instructions. Such companies normally have one director who will be in charge of buildings and new projects and, unless they are developers, they are likely only to do one large project perhaps every five years. They will normally find their architect from direct recommendation of friends, or estate surveyors or other professionals known to them.

The PLC or large corporation

In the large corporate organisation there is usually a department dealing with building headed by a chief engineer or someone of that calibre. They will normally delegate to one of their staff the job of recommending and appointing architects. It is this person who must be sought and found. Often they will put their work out to competition and you will have to make presentations in order to secure it.

In development companies the job of appointing architects is likely to be shared amongst the directors and senior surveyors in the organisation. They will all have their favourite architects and will normally go to them until such time as they leave the company, and then frequently reappoint the same architects when they take up their new position. Their most constant contact is with estate surveyors on whom they rely for a supply of sites and opportunities for development. Therefore the surveyors who advise these developers should also be sought out.

Government bodies

In a local authority, if work is being placed out of house, an architect is appointed by the chief architect or a liaison architect who is chosen by the chief. Local authorities frequently use local architects. The first step therefore is to get yourself on the list of approved architects and then endeavour to meet the appointing architect.

In central government there is a similar system of vetting architects and putting them on an approved list. This is no guarantee of securing work. A superintending architect is probably the person who will appoint outside architects, and he must be sought out through the channels of bureaucracy.

The Property Services Agency (PSA) has instituted a method of competition which requires architects to submit presentations for work with fee competition. In this case the objective is to be on that list and to be asked.

How work can be secured

You can never feel secure with any client. Clients are human and always subject to outside influences. To secure work with an existing client you must be in continual contact and perform well at all times. A quite trivial event not amounting to negligence can end a relationship of many years. Clients can forget all the good work you have done in the past and go to another architect. You can only secure work by having an on-going policy of seeking work, backed up by a practice that can demonstrate a high standard of performance.

If you are being considered by a client for a project, it is really up to you to find the best means of securing the job for yourself.

When the client asks you to make a presentation, you would normally set out to introduce yourselves as people, describe your track record, and demonstrate your specialist knowledge for the particular job. If the presentation includes ideas for solving particular problems, you will have to convince the client that your ideas are the ones which will solve those problems, and make a lasting impression which will lead to his selecting you for the job.

Another way of securing work, or at least of being considered for it, is to build up long term relationships with clients or potential clients. With this type of relationship the potential client should have acquired a good background picture of yourself, your firm and its track record relating to his particular need. Although there may be competition, you have an established relationship and it could be possible to secure the job.

THE PROCESS OF FINDING WORK

Researching the market

Whole books have been written about marketing, but essentially you have to analyse and define your objectives, and then set about achieving them. In defining the type of project you want you must be realistic in assessing whether or not you can actually do the work, or can import the expertise, and prove to your future client that you are capable of competently carrying out his project.

Once you have made up your mind that you are competent and experienced, you have to determine from the press, directories, and other sources of information, who is doing that kind of work and is likely to do more, whether there are new areas of growth in this market and if new firms will be needing buildings.

You need to be aware of current and future market situations, and to be confident that the kind of building you are going to pursue is an expanding market in your location. If you cannot get the information you want, it is advisable to find people, such as estate surveyors, statisticians and product marketing consultants, who are experts in that area of the market and get their opinion on the market's future. From these expert sources you will be able to obtain information, a list of organisations, future trends, types of projects which are normally carried out, their size, value and the kinds of fees paid for professional services. Once you have this information and it has been verified against similar information from other sources, you can begin to identify where you must put your efforts.

This operation, if not carefully conducted and specifically targeted, can be a tremendous waste of time and effort on the part of highly paid principals in an office. The care taken in the initial market research activity results in economies in time when entering the next stage.

Selecting building types

Having found the people who are going to build and the type of building on which they will spend money in the future, you then have to decide on the type of building which you are capable of designing and which you wish to secure for your practice. You then get in touch with those firms you now believe will need such buildings in your location or near to one of your branch offices.

Finding out who wants to build

This can be a long and frustrating activity. It involves finding out possible client firms' intentions for expansion or contraction, who will be responsible for implementing these policies and making the decision on the appointment of consultants. In this type of research you need to understand a company's structures, its organisational system, what its objectives and priorities are, and who have been delegated to make the decision on the employment of building consultants. Then you must find out what prospect there is of getting to see these people, and what has to be done to secure an interview.

However, before actually taking the step to set up the interview it is advisable to find out as much as you can about how the company organises its building programme and if there is any prospect at all of getting in and being considered in relation for such work. Otherwise you may see the person who will be involved in new building but your ignorance of his needs would exclude you from future consideration.

Finding out who has work to give in large companies

Questions to be asked in this connection are:

— Who makes decisions to appoint professional consultants? Is it the board of directors, a committee or an individual?
— Do any consultants participate in appointing outside architects?
— How does the company delegate decisions on large or small capital commitments?
— Who do we see? Must all the decision makers be courted to ensure success?
— Is it possible to contact all decision makers? Can it be achieved or must you select the most persuasive people?
— Do our methods of contact and follow-up create any irritation and resistence in the decision makers?
— Is there a process of decision making that could lead to a policy of progressive contacts with decision makers towards a high level final decider?
— In the case of buildings, does the company only build occasionally and therefore an early repeat assignment is unlikely?
— Is there a division in the level of decision making between, say, large capital new buildings, refurbishment and maintenance, and who takes responsibility for each sector?
— Where the company decides to have competitive presentations who compiles the list of practices to participate?
— How frequently do we get on the list, how often do we fail to get on the list, how often do we succeed in winning the job?
— Does the company have a favourite firm of architects and how do we measure up to their performance?
— What benefits can we offer over our main competitor?

— Is there a distinct pattern in how architects are appointed and is there a distinct type of practice frequently chosen?

— Can we learn from this pattern and mould our image to suit the company preference and follow up with performance which guarantees the next job?

Getting to know the client

Your research has now identified the person you must meet. You may have to employ various techniques to get to that person, i.e. by telephone, by writing, by meeting them at conferences or securing a personal introduction. Once you have met the person it is worth developing a relationship which could be long term before any work opportunity materialises. By that time you should know the person well and have a good insight into how his company functions and how he organises his building programmes and how he feels about the company and its objectives. After many meetings, you should have ensured that your prospective client knows you well, trusts you and your judgment, is aware of what you do in practice, having attended one of your building openings or foundation laying ceremonies, and is aware of your possible future usefulness to his company. From your acquaintanceship with this person you should also endeavour to have some understanding of the internal politics within his company. The age and attitudes of your future client should be studied carefully. If there is a substantial age gap between you and the client, it may be sensible to introduce that person to another member of your practice who may have a closer age relationship and probably interests too.

Making proposals

If you have succeeded so far and the client has at last asked you to make a proposal, you must then call upon your expertise at making presentations, attending interviews, and directly selling the services of your practice. For this purpose someone in your practice should have attended courses on marketing, presentations, and effective speaking. Knowledge and practice of these activities are essential to carrying out this task well and we will now consider the main procedures for an effective presentation.

The first thing in a presentation is to agree on your own agenda and this should be handed to the appraisal committee as soon as you have made your introduction. Once an agenda has been agreed, in planning out the presentation you have to deal with three dimensions of person to person contact. They are:

— The common ground between you and the client.
— The benefits you are offering.
— The message you want them to retain.

A typical agenda might be as follows:

— How you perceive the project.
— Advantages of employing your practice.
— Proposed solutions to client's brief.
— Methods of implementation.
— Fees and methods of payment.

It is advisable to keep the agenda short and absolutely clear.

In order to be proficient at presentations there are a number of points to be borne in mind:

(1) You must give a resumé of your practice:
     (a) Your experience as a practice.
     (b) The experience of your project architect and team.
     (c) Your methods of working through projects.
     (d) How you keep to programmes and cost.
     Your key qualities that have to be put over are your integrity, creativity, reliability and consistency.

(2) You need to ensure that this information is correct by carrying out a company audit. Making sure that you always have on hand details about your staff, the history of projects executed, examples on how you manage time, cost and technology.

(3) You should have a checklist available to ensure that you can relate them to your immediate market situation:
     (a) Location of the project.
     (b) Services required.

(c) Building type required.
(d) Client category.
(e) Size of contract.
(f) Repeat business.
(g) New business.

This checklist should then lead you to your information storage system which must be of immediate accessibility. The information can be available as project sheets, technical data sheets, career summaries, photographs, slides or videos.

The assessment of a presentation will largely depend on the skill of the organisers and their assessment panel. Sometimes it is totally client based without consultants. Or there can be clients and consultants, particularly project managers from different building disciplines. Some research has shown that clients generally reach their decision by giving the following weighting to factors:

Experience and creativity: 50%.
Project people: 30%.
Management: 20%.

The fee does not always have a significant influence because the client will normally not discuss fees in detail until he has decided on the firm he wants to work with.

If you are faced with a presentation you can follow through the normal management processes described in Chapter 1.

(1) Forecast what you are generally aiming at.
(2) Plan out your programme and tasks to be done.
(3) Decide on the staff and materials to be used.
(4) Get your people enthusiastic and willing to put in an extra effort.
(5) Make sure the team works together well.
(6) Set up sensible controls on time and cost — one can be carried away in the excitement of presentations.

You must then decide on what materials of communication are best suited to your presentation. Some of the elements are:

— Data sheets, covers, text pages, photographs, transparencies, drawings, diagrams.

— Various types of illustrations, brochures or booklets which will be left behind with the client to reinforce your proposals and act as a reference system for benefits offered.

You must aim at graphic co-ordination to establish your clear identity, paying particular attention to consistency of logo, colour, type, layout, drawings, illustrations and brochures.

Finally it is useful to know in advance the location of your presentation and to ensure that you have the appropriate visual aids which you know how to work. It is vital to ensure that if you rely on any electrical or mechanical aid, you have a reserve appliance. A well planned presentation can be a disaster if something breaks down or fails to start at the right time.

Some well tried visual aids are: flip charts, display boards, models, overhead projectors, slides, video, films, or chalk or felt pen boards (if you want to do something which appears to be spontaneous).

When you have made your choice have a rehearsal and particularly check the effect of your presentation in relation to position of assessors, time, attention time on one subject, order of display, control of lightness and darkness in the room (particularly when changing, say, from slides to people talking without visual aids) methods of assembling your display and leaving the presentation room.

Finally give everyone in your team a duty for the presentation and for jobs leading up to and after the presentation, go smoothly in and out. Be early, do not fiddle around with anything that is likely to irritate the assessors, but do not be too slick. It can sometimes have an undesired effect.

End up with a smile, thanking the appraisal committee for the opportunity and expressing enthusiasm to do the job for them.

The common ground between you and the client
You should take advantage of the research you have done to ensure you are conversant with the client's needs and that you have already established the common ground between you.

At the beginning of the interview you are likely to meet not only the appointor but also some of his colleagues who are linked with the project and who have also to be convinced that you are the right architect for the job. It is essential that these new people be immediately impressed by the appearance of yourself and your team, and this will happen when you first shake hands, open the agenda and explain what you are going to do during the presentation. These first impressions can lead to success or disaster in seconds.

When everyone has settled down it is important to make up your mind where you want the client to sit in relation to your presentation, whether you wish to be face to face, or side by side. Then the presentation should proceed as planned and rehearsed.

Benefits to be offered

In showing the client what you feel he wants from you you have to make it quite clear what your firm does, how you approach problems, the success of your previous projects, the services you offer, how you solve problems with and away from the client, and you have to show that you have the right team to achieve the client's objective in a harmonious relationship. You may decide at the presentation that there is one point which must be enriched so that the message can be reinforced in the minds of the appraising committee.

The message you wish to leave

This is a total of the personnel, track record and problem solving ability, conveyed to the client in such a way that he will believe you are the best firm he has seen, you suit his style of working, and he will get on well with you, and like the quality of your work.

If you are not asked to make a presentation but to attend a meeting, you will still have to go through most of the procedures required for a presentation. The interview may be less formal and the emphasis more likely on whether the client feels he can get on with you and likes your team.

Getting the commission

After the presentation or interview, if you are successful you will be asked to see the client again. He will want to tell you the good news that you have been selected and at this particular interview you must make the client feel that you care about doing a good job.

The client may want to see one of your buildings before making his final decision. In this case the choice of building must be one most likely to appeal to the client. If you have a satisfied client who is prepared to put himself out in organising such a visit, it is usually advisable to prepare for the visit in advance.

The last part of the sale will be the agreement of terms of engagement. Agreements are now mostly subject to negotiation. Clients want the most competitive percentage or a lump sum fee. Your whole effort could be undone by badly managing this negotiation, perhaps by emphasising extra services or insisting on a very long complicated contract document to be signed showing lack of flexibility on expenses or another trivial matter of costs. Flexibility in first agreeing the basic strategic fee and then making it clear that all other charges are of minor cost can secure the job for you. Avoid any vagueness, agree firm percentages of final construction cost or a lump sum with or without expenses; if these are queried have a round figure available for expenses on a similar job.

CONTROLLING THE OFFICE'S MARKETING PERFORMANCE

The foregoing marketing strategies and techniques are really applicable to firms of a size which can afford to employ people on these activities. Most small practices cannot put such resources into this work. A later part of this chapter summarises a number of ways in which the small practice can get work. But for the office which has resources to carry out marketing activities, these must be managed from within the office.

Policy and planning

A practice with a clear marketing policy will have a senior person in charge who must be given the authority, responsibility and accountability by the partners or company board to set up a department dealing with marketing and sales operations. In the medium sized practice this work will be the responsibility of a partner or director, with probably an associate as assistant. Both of them will also work on projects.

In a very large practice this is a full time job for partner or director with a team of people who will be continuously at work on marketing and sales operations.

Planning and marketing strategies and tactics have to be analysed and planned so that there are targets for the team members to attain. Work types and contacts have to be recorded and monitored on a continuing basis. There should be a measuring system set up with monthly reviews to see if targets are being reached. The essential tools of marketing, such as brochures, press releases, CV's and special medium material, must be assembled and immediately available.

Staffing

There should be a permanently employed marketing team in any large practice of over 100 persons. A partner, associate and an assistant are needed on a full time basis for under 100 persons. Practices of under 50 persons would have one particular partner or director responsible for organising the marketing effort and regularly reporting back to the partners or board of directors. Practices below ten persons will rely on the principal being involved in most of the marketing effort.

Financial control

All practices must have a marketing and entertainment budget. All costs should be recorded and analysed to see whether certain types of marketing expenditure are achieving results. Systems can also identify those efforts which have failed, and resources should no longer be put in this direction.

Those starting a marketing and entertainment policy could well look at their annual expenditure audit, obtain the figures from this source and thereafter set up budgets and targets for expenditure in this field.

More sophisticated management techniques can be employed by targeting certain areas, recording meticulously the cost and effort put into those areas, and measuring results, then showing these results in the various forms of communicable diagrams and charts. This sophistication is probably only for the very large practice.

The marketing effort of the whole office

Everyone in a practice is interested in how new projects come to the office. Regular discussions on marketing and selling can produce rewards, and junior people can develop an understanding of the activity.

MARKETING AND SELLING FOR THE SMALL PRACTICE

For those practices without the resources for large scale marketing it is best to look at the kind of activities that you can include in your working life, moments of relaxation and community relations.

Local direct advertising

Architects may now advertise but although this relaxation in the codes of practice is to be welcomed advertising is a very expensive activity. However the local newspaper is not expensive and may be a fruitful source of advertising for small practices providing local services.

Exhibitions and films

If you have a local library which has an exhibition room, or your office has a large entrance hall, you can set up exhibitions of your work of public interest, in which you can include some examples of your own buildings. This can bring the general public to your office or, if it is a local library, people in your locality will know about your work.

Notice boards on buildings

This is an essential for every architect. Some do not put their notice boards on their buildings and lose the opportunity for publicity. If you are doing an interesting building you can arrange for visits from interested parties and, as they leave the building, they see your board and perhaps remember the name.

Client publicity, letting plans, openings

When you have a project which is of civic interest or is for a charity, you can suggest a foundation laying ceremony which would help fund raising and also draw attention to you as the architect. The same principle applies to topping out or opening a building. Development clients want simplified letting plans. It is worth doing these plans for no charge, as long as you get credit in the brochure which is circulated by the estate agent.

Plaques on finished buildings

Why not put up a plaque to give credit to your client, the builder, consultants and yourself. It can be an impressive testament to the quality of work you can produce.

Competitions

Small practices should go in for competitions which are within their scope and expertise and which, if they win such competitions, can lead to their getting a commission and seeing a project through to completion.

Students and recently qualified architects frequently go in for competitions which they may win but have not the means to execute. In this case the winning of the competition can be an introduction to a partnership which could then be developed and form the basis of the individual's future professional career.

Brochures

In a small practice the cost of brochures can be prohibitive but there is no reason why you should not have a small brochure which you can carry with you and hand out at conferences or any gathering of interested persons, to give a brief introduction to your practice and what it can do for them.

Lecturing

Solicited or unsolicited lectures on interesting architectural topics, to environmental, Civic Trust or corporate societies brings your name into the media, society newsletters and often local papers before and after the lecture has been delivered. Regular lecturing can keep your name in the public eye.

Lecturing in colleges of architecture or evening schools can lead to new contacts which can establish an expertise in the selected field in which you may have clients coming to you as a consultant.

You can also write newspaper and magazine articles on subjects which may interest you or the general public. You can get an appointment to an editorial board or write regular articles on a weekly or monthly basis. This activity has brought many architects into the public and professional eye and has led to the development of many practices.

Serving on conservation committees and architects' panels

Your local authority frequently requires independent, but interested views on the quality of architecture which is being considered for planning permission in your locality. Serving on these committees brings you into contact with local authority officials and councillors, and thus in turn can lead to work.

Civic societies and historic building societies

Many architects interest themselves in the Civic Trust and societies such as the Georgian Society, Victorian Society etc. They can become public figures by becoming chairmen of those societies or giving lectures on behalf of the societies to the general public or acting as expert witnesses in public inquiries, supporting a local view, perhaps on an infrastructure plan presented by the local authority for public approval.

Politics

If you are interested in politics but do not wish to be involved at a national level, you can stand as a parish councillor or local government councillor and become known for your activities and a familiar name in your borough or district.

Family involvement

Your family can be a useful source of contacts for your practice. Introductions, recommendations, social occasions can be arranged so that you can meet people who may want to use your services. This can be achieved in a relaxed informal atmosphere which is often the beginning of a long term relationship with a client.

Old school and college friends

When you leave school it might be sensible to join the Old Pupils Association. You can play for them in their sporting activities, attend their fetes and be a committee member. These contacts are often useful particularly as you get older and your old school colleagues are promoted into positions where they may wish to employ an architect.

Membership of clubs and associations

Every town has its clubs and associations and the larger ones their professional institutes. Your membership of clubs, Rotary, Working Men's Clubs, Conservative Clubs, golf clubs, Round Tables etc can bring you in touch with a wide variety of people in commercial and industrial areas who could possibly become future clients.

Joining local religious organisations

Many architects have started their careers by being asked to assist the local church, mosque, synagogue etc in carrying out extensions or perhaps building a new religious centre. Your regular attendance at your religious community gatherings can often lead to long term friendships and business relationships.

Working for charities

By joining committees who are fund raising for charities you can widen your contacts, show people your management skills, participate in a worthwhile team activity and meet people who could give you work.

Participation in sports

A large proportion of the population now carry out activities to keep themselves fit by joining sports clubs. You can meet people outside your profession who may progress inside their own companies and eventually be in a position to decide on the appointment of an architect.

Relationships with other professionals

If you work in an isolated region or solely in a local borough it is worth getting friendly with local solicitors, accountants, insurance brokers, who are often requested to recommend architects or other professionals by their clients.

Relations with other building consultants

It pays to get on well with the other consultants in the building team, and for you to recommend other consultants who have proven their value by good performance, and to encourage those whom you recommend to recommend you.

Regular rendezvous

Find out where local estate agents or businessmen gather after a day's work. Local pubs, clubs or restaurants are frequently chosen being close to the centre of activity. Get friendly with one of the gathering and let him introduce you to the others. The only snag is that you have to turn up regularly or they will forget you.

It is unlikely in a small practice that you could carry out every activity listed above but if you select those you find can be easily done by you and from which you would derive enjoyment, why not try and see if it produces the desired results.

RELATIONSHIPS WITH THE PRESS AND THE MEDIA

You may come into contact with the media for a variety of reasons:

(1) Your building is in the news and information is needed immediately.
(2) You or your clients are involved in, say, a topping out ceremony and you want to prepare a press release about the building and the people.
(3) You are asked to appear on TV or speak on radio either as immediate news or for a prepared programme.
(4) You are involved in a public planning inquiry or meeting

and you will present evidence which will be seen by the press who are in attendance.

When faced with any of these situations it is vital not to let the experts take you over.

Try at all times to have available clear, concise information on data sheets. The press in its haste won't read through extensive text, but they can extract facts if you give them clearly. They will interpret the facts to make their own points which make a story for them.

If the press get your story wrong this is unfortunate. Even if you get them to apologise in their paper, it will be in small print, on the least read page, but even bad news is better than no news. The interview on radio or TV can be quite intimidating — the best way to ensure success is to attend a course on speech making and interviewing.

See yourself on video answering questions under pressure, see how you present illustrations, listen to the criticisms and practise until you feel confident. You must remember that most radio or TV interviews are very short, they have to be packed with facts, and edited with no redundancy. When being interviewed on TV let them make up your face and follow their advice on presentation methods. Confidence is vital for getting over your point. Most architects who appear on TV seem to come over as diffident mumblers.

3 Establishment of an office

When I lecture to students, particularly in their final year, I ask how many of the students would like to start off in practices on their own once they have obtained sufficient experience. Normally in a class of 30 about five raise their hands. Out of that five it is possible that only one will succeed but it is more likely that they will all fail. In recent surveys of architects' offices, when the question was asked 'How did your practice start?' it was found that there are various ways:

(1) By inheriting a practice from family or close friends.
(2) By buying a practice.
(3) By working your way up in a small firm to a partnership.
(4) By winning a competition and starting on your own.
(5) By being given a project and starting on your own.
(6) By starting on your own without any projects and ghosting for other architects until you start to get projects of your own.
(7) By partners starting up together and by one principal starting on his own and others buying a share in the partnership as it develops.
(8) By joining a group practice and getting work first from your colleagues and then finding time to go out and get your own clients and projects.
(9) By joining a co-operative and sharing work and costs.

Irrespective of how the principals started in their practice it is obvious that the prime means by which a practice can be established are the availability of money and work.

A few architects are fortunate in inheriting a substantial sum of money and can set up a small practice in a desirable location and then go out and seek work and be prepared to live off their capital for a few years until the practice is established. This luxury is not available to most architects, as generally speaking those who start out on their own with a small amount of work have little money and therefore work from home. If they are successful they will expand into a separate office in due course. The biggest task facing a new office is the continuation of work load and income.

There are some practical steps which must be taken before even these problems can be tackled. They are as follows:

(1) Finding the premises.
(2) Leasing or owning premises.
(3) Establishment of a business name.
(4) Furnishing and equipping the office.
(5) Making your existence known to others.

Finding premises

Many architects commence practice from their home. After all, they only need a room, a desk, a drawing board and a telephone. All other services can be sub-contracted or delegated. This arrangement has a number of advantages and disadvantages.

On the positive side you waste no time travelling between home and work so normally, except for interruptions from the telephone and odd callers you can concentrate on your work, and can usually work at any hour you like without disturbing others. This can be a very flexible arrangement.

However, there are also many disadvantages. All small chores which would normally be done by a secretary or assistant have to be done by yourself — getting prints, posting letters, making telephone calls, finding telephone numbers, doing your own book-keeping etc. When you leave the house there is nobody to receive calls. Most people do not like to leave messages on an answering machine. When you go on holiday everything stops.

Some of the disadvantages can be overcome by having your wife, husband or a friend who is prepared to look after your administration on a part time basis, but then their payment out of your fee income may be too heavy a burden, particularly in the early stages of practice. As the one-person practice develops into a full time job, the decision of whether to grow or remain as you are will have to be taken. Those wishing to occupy premises outside their homes then have to search for a suitable office.

Leasing offices

Normally a small practice cannot afford its own self-contained offices. Therefore they either have to be shared, in a cheap form of accommodation over a shop, in an existing house shared by other professionals, or in a few spare rooms in a small office building which may be surplus to a lessee's requirements.

Finding these premises can be time consuming and difficult. The best means of finding accommodation is to go to estate agents to find out the rentals for the various types of accommodation and what is available locally. It is sometimes useful to look at local newspapers to find what may be vacant at a low price on a short term lease. Estate agents can cause much time wasting as they often offer offices which have been on their books for long periods and have proved unsatisfactory to prospective occupiers. It is important to be positive with estate agents in order to ensure that they do not waste your time looking at unsuitable premises.

Generally speaking, when practices are starting up, they are looking for cheap, easily accessible premises in a respectable location. It is unusual for clients to visit small practices; normally the individual practising architect visits his clients' premises.

The minimum size suite is usually two drawing offices and one administrative office; the rooms should be of sufficient size to allow for expansion of up to five persons in the practice before another move is contemplated. This is particularly important if it is the policy of the principal to go for growth.

Even though at this stage of the practice's life money is in short supply, it is advisable to have the aid of a solicitor in negotiating your lease and if you have a friendly surveyor to have his assistance in negotiating the rent. Your accountant should also be consulted regarding allowances and other tax advantages which are available when starting up in business, particularly government allowances and grants which are available in some parts of the country.

Considerable patience has to be exercised in waiting for solicitors of both sides to agree a contract and terms of the lease. The time which elapses is worth using in expanding your business and progressing your present situation and not wasting time in the futile and frustrating activity chasing solicitors and others.

If you have a full repairing lease it is particularly important to have a proper schedule of dilapidations and agree the standard of the interior and exterior of the building. You will then not be faced with large costs at the end of the lease or when you want to assign it.

If you have plenty of capital and wish to buy your office, occupying part of the building and sub-letting the rest, there are fairly straightforward matters which have to be covered.

Ownership of premises

The advantage of ownership, of course, is that if you buy outright you have less of a cash flow problem later on as you are not paying for your lease, but may indeed be collecting rent, and you have the flexibility of expanding into your own premises as and when necessary. It is therefore important that any leases or licences should have a six month break clause which allows you to reoccupy their part of the premises without hindrance. You cannot expect to recover the full market rent from sub-letting part of the premises. Moreover the income from such leases is heavily taxed and does not really constitute a good source of revenue. The advantages are those of having expandable space available on the same premises with the resultant saving in cost of moving from one premises to another and the maintenance of a stable address which also has certain advantages to clients.

Renting shared space

Another way to start up in practice is to join a shared facilities group practice. This is normally set up by a group of professional people, such as architects, quantity surveyors and engineers, who are starting off on their own and who rent rooms in a building, with one room for administration manned by a secretary/ receptionist. Members of the practice pay rent for their own room, and share costs, overheads, and the cost of keeping a secretary and the administration room available for all members of the group. Usually all members are directors of an unlimited company which owns the building lease and common furniture and fittings. Those who do not want to be directors pay a monthly tenancy charge with a break clause. A shared facilities group practice is an economical way to start, or it can act as a half way house between practising at home and setting up your own office.

Advantages

The advantages are that you have your independence while sharing with others the cost of the services and facilities. Depending on the type of building you occupy you will either have a room or a certain amount of space for which you pay rent. Often the other members of the practice can be available to help you out when you have a heavy workload.

Disadvantages

There are also disadvantages in this form of practice normally based on the problems of expansion and contraction of workload which is experienced by the members, the movement of people in and out of the group practice for either expansion or failure, the problems of sharing out the work by the administrator and the way in which the administrator costs each person's time and the speed in which the service works for each individual, particularly when there are complaints that the administrator is favouring one person over another.

From observation of group practices it is unusual for anyone to stay for more than about five years and therefore there must be a sound system for dealing with the constant movements and changes and meeting the overhead cost on a fairly shared basis.

Working communities

Another type of accommodation is the renting of work space in a working community. The advantages to residents of the working community are manifold. There is a fully prepared space ready for occupation. There are no difficulties over leases, telephones, renovations or the ability to expand or contract the size of the space. There are lower overheads because of shared facilities like reception, intercom, telex, conference rooms, technical library and a restaurant. There is a manager available to look after heating, lighting, maintenance and cleaning, and there is the advantage of working in close proximity to others who could either be customers, helpers or suppliers.

Working communities are often found in locations which are in declining neighbourhoods where the local authority is encouraging job creation schemes. Here they will give a grant and rent free periods in order to encourage this type of use of what would normally be cheap warehouse or old factory accommodation.

Community workshops have not been going long enough to really assess their acceptability and viability. They are really a more sophisticated form of the shared facility practice and people are likely to have the same experiences as with this form of shared accommodation.

THE SMALL PRACTICE

The small architectural practice usually operates from home, in rented premises over shops or in part of an older house on the fringe of a town centre.

Staffing of this kind of practice might consist of a part two architectural assistant and a technical draughtsperson undergoing part-time training at a local college. Typing is undertaken by a part-time secretary working from home. Book-keeping and accounts may be done by the principal, a spouse or part-time book-keeper. Everyone shares the duties of handling the post, answering the telephone, filing, getting prints and making tea.

The principal spends most of his time out of the office running a number of small jobs with poorly organised builders, and going to meetings of local organisations in order to meet new clients.

The staff find it difficult to get instructions from their principal because there is always a rush. There is no job costing or control, the cash position being usually checked by looking at a bank statement or the cheque book. Programming is not done on a regular basis, and the assistants learn to cope with crises and changing of drawings and much overtime for the sake of the 'happy family'.

A variation of this type of structure can be seen when two architects get together in a partnership. Often, one of the partners is a part-time lecturer and a good designer and 'desk man', while the other is a practical manager and job getter. Their problem is still the same: money and time to get the work done. They often employ part-time self employed staff and have a few local ghosters when the 'heat' is on. Generally they do not do any management accounting or programming but live from day to day in a surge of activity or come to a full stop realising there is no work to be done. This I call a part-time partnership.

TYPICAL TRADITIONAL GROWING SMALL OFFICE

This structure is probably representative of the majority of practices in Great Britain. The practice is accommodated in an extension to the principal's house or in a shop or small house near the other professional practices on the fringe of the town centre. Often the practice has been purchased from an architect who wished to retire, or is a part of a split partnership, or has been started from scratch by the principal.

The administration is run by a mature person who works very hard, does many administrative duties and menial chores, with plenty of overtime for free. The principal is out most of the time, and the associate is expected to run the office while the principal is away. The staff are set tasks mainly by the associate on behalf of the principal who will from time to time get directly involved on 'the board'.

The associate hopes one day to become a partner but the pressure of the job only allows time for occasional evening contacts for securing jobs. The other assistants can be a mixture of full-time unqualified draughtspersons, technicians doing part-time study, a part two architect, or a self-employed qualified architect.

One of the major problems is that workload fluctuates. This is true of all practices, but in the small practice, which is perhaps faced with a delay in an important job or a government cutback affecting a type of work, this can have a major effect on the practice's stability. Often the small practice uses outside labour for ghosting to act as a cushion for those busy times which all too often end abruptly when a work source dies before another can be born.

The stable small practice is the foundation of the country's architectural service. Such practices are seldom run as profit oriented organisations, but they cannot afford to have too many loss-making years. Therefore good management principles should be translated into a common sense, balanced approach to business.

THE GROWING SMALL PRACTICE

Small practices aiming at growth will probably set up slightly different structures in order to achieve their objectives. At the earlier stages they should create a proper business management system. The principals will be mainly concerned with getting more work, while the assistants are there to see that the projects are properly run and completed at the right cost, on time and to the desired design.

The essence of the growing small practice is mobility. It may have to move offices from time to time to accommodate the increase in workload. Consequently, the growing office must be more efficiently structured than the rather static local small firm.

In the small practice it is advisable that the principal and the staff should meet at least once a week, with a standard agenda, to go through the normal discussions and decision making required for that particular office. Because the future of the office will be founded on a good delegation system, minutes (if thought necessary) should be properly recorded and action should be seen to be effective. At monthly meetings there should be a simple column type budgetary system and a system for measuring job profitability.

Financial information may not be readily available on a monthly basis, but should be provided on at least a quarterly basis by the part-time book-keeper. Most of the decision making relating to staff, projects etc. can be made on a day to day basis because of the small size of the office, which allows everyone to see each other at some time during a week. This is not always the case in the larger offices.

Financial control must be continuous because the growing practice normally is borrowing money up to its limit and therefore its efficiency must be greater to achieve a reasonable profit whilst paying high interest charges.

ORGANISATION STRUCTURES

Key:

A — Assistant. Acc — Accounts. Assoc — Associate. BK — Book-keeper. **COMP** — Computer. CP/T — Computer technician. D — Director. **JA** — Job Architect. **JP/D** — Junior Partner or Director. LIB — Librarian. **OM** — Office Manager. **P** — Principal. **P/T** — Part time. RCP — Receptionist. **SA** — Senior Assistant. **Sec** — Secretary. T — Technician. Te — Team. TYP — Typist

SMALL PRACTICES

"Happy Family"

Part-Time Partnership

Typical growing small practice

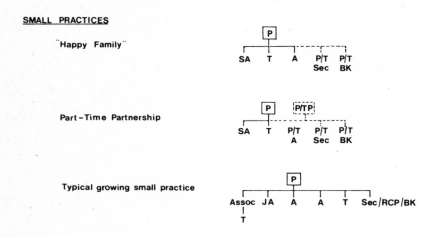

MEDIUM SIZED PRACTICES

Principal and two Junior Partners / Directors

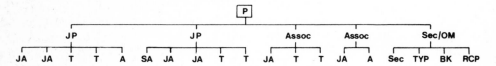

Two equal Partner/Directors

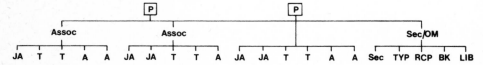

LARGE CENTRALISED PRACTICE

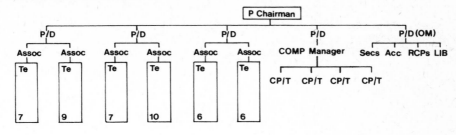

Corporate responsibilities of partners & associates

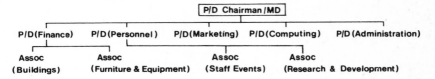

VERY LARGE DECENTRALISED PRACTICE WITH BRANCHES

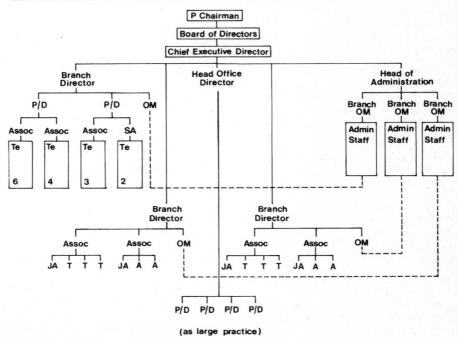

While my practice was growing from 3 to 33 persons I never had a bank statement that was in the 'black'. During the 1960s and early 1970s businesses worked on the principle of expanding on other people's money, for interest was low, but nowadays this has been rejected as inflationary. Whilst the current monetary philosophies prevail and interest rates are above 10 per cent, it will be harder for small practices to expand. Happily there are always the exceptions which break all rules and make rapid progress to success despite the current constraints.

In the growing small practice much time is wasted by all getting information and doing chores, and site visits are more necessary because of the size of jobs and efficiency of the builders. Some management accounting and programming can be done by the associate but often this is frustrated by the principal overriding everything for expediency. Despite these failings they are often happy offices with everyone contributing to the regular crises, often for little financial reward, but good morale and attitudes to work are an important part in the office life. Such practices may be static either because of a conscious decision on the part of the principal or because of market conditions.

If there is a policy for growth then the principal in a small practice must exercise the vital skill of delegation. If successful, more work will come in, the practice will grow and greater management specialisation will be necessary.

THE MEDIUM SIZED OFFICE

Most medium sized offices are in large cities or their environs. They usually number between 10 and 25 people and have approximately three or four principals and two or three associates. They are either partnerships or unlimited companies, and there are now a few limited companies. Most medium sized practices have been in existence for many years and there is usually quite a wide age range throughout the office. Normally they have a client base stable enough to ensure that they stay around the same size, irrespective of external events, as long as the principals are actively engaged in serving clients and developing new opportunities.

The first essential is that the objectives of the office must be clear. The larger the number of people involved in the direction of the partnership or company, the more important it becomes to set straightforward objectives, with a clear office structure and everyone's duties clearly specified. There can be noticeably different structures in offices of this size, depending on the way in which work is handled. This will be the subject of a separate chapter.

The temptation to have too many levels of responsibility must be avoided. It is no longer possible to have a happy family structure and to deal with matters affecting the whole practice on a day to day basis as in the small practice. Regular meetings and methods of communication must be established in order to retain the objectivity of the practice and to carry out the policies which normally have to be written and defined more clearly than in the smaller practices.

Often a medium sized office will have sufficient cash flow and funds to buy their own premises. This is by far the best means of ensuring a good capital base. However, it has often been argued that renting property releases working capital for improvements to the architectural services and the directors must then decide on the importance of location, as they may not necessarily agree about the most favoured choice for accessibility to and for clients.

In the medium sized practice the overhead percentage can make the difference between loss and profit and must be given detailed attention. The heady expenditure of the 1960s and 70s is over and a more frugal regime is now necessary for survival. However, on a more positive note the growing medium sized practice has more confidence in tackling the task of trying to convince anxious bank managers that there is future growth in the business when the overall climate in the building industry is contrary to this trend.

The structure

The diagram on page 38 shows the structure of a typical medium sized practice, with the sole principal forming a partnership or a limited or unlimited company in which there is a majority shareholder.

Delegation exists in two sectors:

(1) By jobs
(2) Corporate.

Job delegation entails the three or so partners or directors meeting regularly to decide who carries out the projects within the office and is responsible throughout. Staff will be allocated to the partner/director according to the programmed office workload and need in special circumstances. The partner/director will have the authority, responsibility and accountability for the performance of his delegated projects. Clients may also be allocated to partners/directors for work continuity and public relations.

Corporate management means that partners/directors must accept responsibilities for finance, accounting, personnel, production, design policy, contract policy, marketing, administration, property etc.

In a medium sized practice a director in charge of corporate management is not economically viable. Therefore these duties have to be shared out among the partners/directors. It is often a good idea to rotate the duties, say, every three years unless somebody is temperamentally unsuited to a task.

There must be a high management input in a medium sized practice. There should be an established job cost control system, weekly job allocation procedures and programming of work, co-ordinated project programmes and timetables, cash flow and liquidity forecasts, fee monitoring and management, marketing budget and strategy, monthly debit and credit statements, quarterly financial statements and budget checks. A typical planning and co-ordinating meeting is held in my office every Monday morning from 9.30 to 10.30. A typical agenda is noted below. The meeting achieves the objective of every member of staff knowing what is going on inside and outside the practice.

Agenda for weekly office meeting
(1) Introduction of new staff.
(2) Staff resources allocation to projects this week.
(3) Computer staff utilisation.
(4) Future staff allocations.
(5) Information on new projects in feasibility stage.
(6) Report from travelling clerk of works on building quality and defects.
(7) Report on new publications by librarian.
(8) Future market trends.
(9) Any other business.

All of these systems should be subject to weekly, monthly or quarterly assessments as deemed necessary for the proper control and direction of the practice. Projects are usually not large or frequent enough to keep a team system so there must be staff flexibility to enable movement from one to another in need of support. Teams under an associate are too inflexible for small projects. People have to be delegated to other teams in the practice too frequently to establish any team identity.

Some medium sized practices are set up with equal partners and the diagram on page 38 shows a typical structure. With this arrangement there must be extra attention to unity of objectives otherwise the firm can be split in two and there will be battles between the partners for key staff. If there are three equal partners then there must be some voluntary arrangement for an annual senior partner in rotation to make final decisions.

THE LARGE OFFICE

Most large offices are found in the larger cities. Their staff can be anything from 25 to 500. They have normally been established for many years, usually having been set up by an outstanding architect. In some cases the outstanding architect has died or retired and has now left a corporate entity to continue and expand the office's services. The firm may have become multi-disciplinary and have branch offices throughout the country. It is a corporation and its size demands that there are senior managers responsible for its proper functioning as a corporate entity without any direct project responsibility.

Depending on the numbers engaged, the partners or directors can number up to 20 persons. They may be scattered throughout the country and abroad, and will not be able to see each other on a regular basis. Probably those from the more remote offices will meet only once a quarter or each half year. There may be two levels of management, one to deal with the overall objectives and policies, the other with executive responsibilities.

The practice may need many specialist departments or companies operating under separate names to identify different types of service. All these have to be defined and clearly understood in terms of the office structure, which would be the responsibility of an office manager or director who would be solely occupied in making sure that the organisation functions efficiently.

Branch offices will have their own sub-structures related to the overall structure. It will be the office manager's duty to see that communication channels are open and that there is a reasonably flexible reaction system to changes which occur both externally and internally.

There could be monthly branch office and main board meetings and a system of weekly board meetings may be necessary in order to ensure that the organisation functions as a single unit. More time has to be devoted by all persons in this type of organisation to the proper management of the various parts and their co-ordination into a unified and efficient service.

Consequently the larger office has the problem of creating a bureaucracy which works down to grass roots level. This is a difficult management task which confronts all engaged in running a successful enterprise of this nature.

There are however some basic rules:

— Design your structure with as few levels as practicable and keep relationships direct and personal.
— Set up good communication systems which ensure unity of objective for everyone serving the practice.
— Use all the available management aids for financial control.
— Keep your marketing and advertising effective and not too sloppily widespread.
— Stay in one building in the same city. Only have branches for geographical reasons?
— Set up systems to keep your middle managers (job architects) in focus. Large firms have much trouble if middle managers are not kept informed at all times.
— Have a training scheme for junior members of the office and encourage them to become experts at something which will benefit the practice's services.
— Keep in the forefront of technological progress and give a lead where possible in a particular area of the architects' work where it pays off in publicity.
— Make sure that with all this structural care you do not forget the senior partners' or directors' personal relationships, their image, recognition, standing in society, and other strategic representational roles which are linked with the image of your practice and their personal esteem is at stake.

THE VERY LARGE PRACTICE

The very large practice with branches at home and abroad will require a more sophisticated management structure based on whole branch delegation and profit centres with financial allocations and other fiscal control and performance criteria. A typical structure is shown in the diagram on page 39.

To manage such a large and complicated enterprise is beyond the scope of this book. Needless to say however, it requires architects and managers of the highest quality to ensure success.

On the main board there may be two non executive directors appointed by the supporting bank or an insurance company who have a stake in the firm.

There would be three director levels:

(1) The Board
(2) Executive
(3) Local structure.

The board would only deal with major strategy, policy, financial and organisation matters.

The executive board would deal with the strategy and policy of branches, interpreting and organising implementation throughout the branches. They would set targets of performance in turnover and profitability. For control purposes they would receive statistical information to report back to the main board.

Branches would implement policy and run their firms in the same way as well run medium sized local practices, incorporating all management systems to achieve targets and control, thus ensuring that targets of time, money and client satisfaction are achieved.

Whatever size of practice you have, it is unlikely to be static; therefore the structures shown in the chapter are only an aid to good organisation and should be subject to constant change.

GROUP PRACTICES

In the early 1960s many young architects who had qualified after the war had built up enough experience in offices to attempt to practice on their own account. The first problem encountered was lack of money to set up a new office and sustain a regular cash flow until fees began to flow in.

With the lack of money came the inability to employ regular staff and also allow time to meet people and develop new clients.

Architects who had left local authorities and taught in schools of architecture decided to pool their resources and share costs. Some brought in consultants from other building disciplines and they formed shared facilities group practices.

I was a founder member of one of the original group practices. We had a group of architects, engineers and interior designers, all with the same problem. They were trying to practise from home and had teaching or ghosting jobs to keep a steady cash flow. We met together and decided to find premises in a good business location, where rent was cheap, and not too far away from the polytechnic where most of the group taught. The top two floors of a Georgian building were found and an economical rent negotiated. The lease was signed by all nine original members and spaces or rooms were provided for each member who paid a share of the rent and outgoings. One room was reserved for the central administration which was to be staffed by a full time secretary/receptionist/girl Friday. Her salary was paid proportionately on the same basis as the rent, with extra payments per letter produced and telephone calls made by members of the group.

The group practice members formed a committee which had monthly meetings. The meetings were actually board meetings because the accountant had recommended that a service company be set up and all group members became directors. Each director had a corporate responsibility, e.g. finance, accounting, administration, and reported on progress at the monthly meeting. The secretary recorded all costs against the members and an analysis was carried out monthly by the finance and accounting directors.

Once established in their own place, directors bought new furniture and equipment through the company to get the best discounts. They shared the cost of the administration equipment, and subsequently its running costs.

Each member continued in practice with their own clients, sharing the same letterhead if they wished, or using solely their own name. A system for retiring members and the sale of shares to new members was organised, and because of the nature of the practice, some members found the system very satisfactory, whilst others decided to leave.

There were many problems to deal with at every monthly meeting, mainly caused by the situation of nine independent practitioners trying to get the best for themselves out of the group practice.

Some stayed for many years and found group practice just the right system for their work, others failed to continue in work and left because they could not afford to stay, others used the practice as a halfway house to expand their practice and when it became too large for the group, had sufficient funds to launch out on their own.

Group practice suits architects who want to remain in sole charge of their work, with perhaps a few assistants or using other members in project partnerships on a fee sharing basis. However, expansion of one practice in the group causes conflicts and in such a case the architects should move out to an independent practice as soon as their size becomes disproportionate to the rest. Contraction can be accommodated by taking less space and not using the administration to the same degree as others, thereby reducing costs during slack periods.

There are many types of group practices and shared workshops with differing structures, types of premises and people, but the general objective is to share costs and services with others in order to get started in your own practice.

CONSORTIA

Clients for very large projects expect to deal with one representative organisation for all building design and construction services. Projects of this nature are usually overseas in countries where there are no existing organisations large enough to execute the work.

Professionals and contractors form a consortium to meet client requirements. The consortium is led by the contractor or professional practice which will bring the team together in order to make a combined design and build bid.

A consortium agreement is drawn up by solicitors who will endeavour to cover all relevant matters affecting the parties and their relationship. This is a very specialist task and anyone involved should get their own solicitor to ensure that it is fair and reasonable. The crucial factor is how the money is to be shared. Other considerations include when payment is made and how much money is paid up front.

Consortia are very difficult to manage. Commitment from participating practices and contractors requires strong leadership to keep all involved in meeting target dates and costs. All participating have dual allegiances: to their own practices or companies and to the consortium which sometimes gets second priority.

The sharing of costs of establishments overseas is sometimes disproportionate to the amount of financial return achieved. Because the size of the contracts are enormous compared with those in the UK, the initial setting-up costs of the consortium can be a large drain on funds for professional practices before cash flow leads to profit.

4 The legal basis of practice

An architect may exercise his profession in a number of different ways. He may:

(a) practise on his own as an individual
(b) practise with other architects as a partnership, otherwise known as a 'firm'
(c) be the employee of a company
(d) be the employee of a local authority
(e) be the employee of a statutory body
(f) be the employee of another architect
(g) be the employee of a partnership
(h) be 'an associate' of a practice, in which event he is in law a sub-contractor to the practice.

THE INDIVIDUAL ARCHITECT

It is no longer necessary for individuals trading under a name other than their own to register this with the Registrar of Companies. So that Joe Bloggs can trade as 'Joe Bloggs & Company' or 'Joe Bloggs & Associates' or as 'The Most Efficient Architects' without in any way having to register this.

It is, however, still necessary for correspondence and fee notes to disclose the exact ownership of the practice, i.e. Joe Bloggs trading as The Most Efficient Architects.

For income tax purposes, he will be assessed under Schedule D.

A partnership is a relationship which exists between persons carrying on a trade or a profession or a business in common with a view to profit.

A formal partnership agreement in writing is not therefore required and not infrequently the courts have held that there has been a partnership even though one or more of those concerned have vehemently denied it. There can also be a partnership in fact between one or more individuals and one or more companies.

It is, however, prudent for an architect who intends to practise as a partner to enter into a formal partnership agreement in the form of a deed.

A partnership as such has no separate legal personality, although under law it can sue, or be sued, in the firm's name.

The great drawback is that all partners have unlimited liability for the debts and damages that may be awarded against the partnership. Even if one partner was in no way concerned with a project that proves to be defective, he will be held as much liable as the partner who was in fact concerned with it. Moreover, the decisions or conduct of one partner bind all the others.

A partnership comes to an end whenever one partner leaves or dies or a new partner is accepted. This has certain income tax advantages, but it also has difficult legal consequences so far as employment of staff is concerned.

The deed of partnership

If you decide to go into partnership, then it is prudent to draw up a partnership deed. The pitfalls if you do not get your partnership agreement signed are many. It is easy to start working together on an informal basis on new projects with great opportunities. All goes well until an event occurs which strikes at the root of the partnership.

Unless you have specifically covered all possibilities in your partnership agreement you could find yourself paying solicitors' bills and involved in time-consuming litigation for years after the event.

Partners should ensure that the foundation of their business is expressed in writing and that all matters which may affect them

now and in the future are written in to a formal partnership deed.
Some of the points which must be included are as follows.

(1) The full names of the parties to the deed must be clearly
stated with their addresses.

(2) The name under which the firm is to carry on its business
must be agreed.

There is a certain emotional interest in seeing one's name
on the headed paper. It is often regarded as the fulfilment of
many years' ambition. However, if there are many partners
the number of names on the heading may have to be limited
and this can cause disappointment to new partners and affect
their keenness to succeed. Recently we have seen a
depersonalisation of partnership names which avoids this
problem but brings in its wake the problem of the very
ambitious partner who must see his name at the top and
therefore leaves to form his own practice.

The other problem this practice avoids is an argument on
the merger of one partnership with another, when it has to be
decided whose name is first in the list of names, particularly
when the most senior person only has a year or so to
retirement. Many hours of debate can be spent on the name
alone, so reserve some time or get a person who is
independent to suggest suitable names.

(3) The name and address of the place of business must be
included in the deed, including any branch offices which may
be opened from time to time, which must be added to the
deed.

In its early days a partnership may try to appear larger and
more experienced than it is by setting up in associations
round the country, or indeed overseas. Sometimes it may suit
a client to know there is a representative of the partnership,
say in the north if your practice is in the south, but once the
client knows the real situation the ruse tends to fail.

An associate is a member of staff who has been with the
practice for many years and is recognised as having partnership potential. As a half way house and to test the
person's ability at a higher level in the practice, the person

can be called an associate. By putting the person's name on the firm's note paper he has a greater standing in the eyes of clients and the staff.

The associate must not be confused with a full partner and the firm's headed paper must make this clear.

An associate is not responsible for the profits or losses or legal liabilities of the practice and has no legal corporate authority. In my experience about 75 per cent of associates become partners or directors after about five years. If this does not occur by then, it may be better for them to leave the practice.

(4) The date of commencement of the partnership should be entered in the deed, but before this is done an accountant's advice should be sought as it could affect the dates of the partnership's financial year, and consequently affect tax liabilities.

It cannot be emphasised strongly enough that it is essential to have the continuing advice of your solicitor and accountant throughout the period of drawing up a partnership agreement. Taxation is very complex and Budgets regularly change detailed parts of the taxation laws, which in turn can affect your partnership and you may not have picked this up from newspapers or journals. Many accountants send out an annual analysis of the Budget but beware of this as it is usually sent off before the implementing Finance Act has passed through Parliament and there may be amendments which affect you.

(5) The partners will supply capital to the company in agreed proportions, which must be stated in the deed.

This is one of the most intractable parts of the negotiations which has to be settled by the partners alone. Capital in a highly taxed society is indeed hard to acquire and money from savings or even inheritance is not sufficient to meet the high costs of setting up a practice on a sound financial basis.

There are many other ways of raising money for capital and shares through insurance policies, second mortgages, special loans through Government agencies, banks etc. Again your accountant is your best advisor.

(6) There must be provision for further contributions of capital and allowance should be made for the purchase of a share in the existing practice by an incoming partner.

It must always be possible and attractive for a new partner to join the practice. There are many methods of paying into the practice and making provision for a partner leaving and being replaced. Insurances can be taken out to cover the costs of these movements. In this case your accountant and insurance broker should be consulted.

(7) Provision should be made for the withdrawal of capital, particularly in the event of a partner's death or retirement, or if the partnership is dissolved.

If the clauses for this part of the agreement are not clearly stated and vetted carefully by your solicitor, you will rue the day you signed the agreement. Dissolution of a partnership for any reason can be traumatic. Death or retirement of a very active partner can be catastrophic if the clients vanish too.

Taxation comes to the fore in this provision and unless these matters are handled carefully the remaining partners could be carrying a burden of tax for a deceased partner for many years.

When consulting your solicitor and accountant on the phrasing of clauses under this heading it is advisable to think of the worst possible occurrences and make clear provisions. Even then you will not cover everything. Each change in a partnership has something unique about it which requires value judgements and hard decisions.

(8) The value of property or work in hand which is contributed by the individual at the commencement of the partnership has to be transferred to the joint names to constitute part of the partnership's assets. Any special terms concerning the consideration for these transfers have to be defined.

Everyone has an inflated view of the value of their assets. To avoid argument it is better to agree to independent valuations. Where property is concerned it is often jointly owned and if one person leaves the partnership the other partners have to find the money to buy him or her out. If homes are included, joint ownership can have unexpected consequences for the valuations of the property. In the event of divorce the partners' share could radically decrease.

It is always wise to undervalue assets to begin with and then have regular revaluations made at agreed periods. Special terms for assets can relate to trusts and other fiscal arrangements which are made with investments aimed at minimising taxation.

(9) Proportions in which profits or losses are to be shared between the partners should be defined.

This is best left to independent advisors, because unless the situation is simple, partners will never agree, or if they do in order to show flexibility and willingness to collaborate at the start, they may harbour resentments about their leniency at a later date.

(10) The rate of interest to be allowed on capital contributed by the partners should be agreed.

This is always a debatable point and some accountants recommend that interest should not be included. Those with different opinions should be very careful to select a rate of interest which is variable and based on bank rate; if it is decided to have a fixed rate you may regret the choice. In architectural practices there are lean and fat years and the application of high interest payments could cause financial embarrassment.

(11) The amount of notional salaries or cash drawings by each of the partners on a monthly or other basis should be agreed by the partners.

Another very tricky matter for agreement is the question of notional salaries, which are always very difficult to set. Everyone has a different life style and needs differing amounts of money at different stages in their life. Young partners have pensions and savings to build up. Different motives determine notional salary levels, forecasts of partnership income can be wrong and therefore the basis of what can be afforded is lost. Most partners should take low notional salaries and work for good profits and their share of these. It is only the first year which is hard if the practice is successful. The profit share can also be forecast (wrongly of course) and each individual partner can make arrangements with financial sources to tide him over until a consistent income is achieved. You may need an accountant's final decision clause as part of the agreement.

(12) Arrangements should be agreed in connection with banking, auditing accounts and signing cheques.

If the partners are starting up together for the first time they should sign cheques jointly until they have settled into their new roles. An established partnership drawing up a new agreement will probably have an agreed system for cheque signing. The arrangements with the bank depend on your ability to communicate to the bank manager the nature and financial needs of your business. Usually one partner has these skills and so this task should be delegated to that person.

The annual audit should be done by your accountant who would take your instructions and advise you on the best methods of presentation.

(13) The responsibilities and duties of the partners have to be defined in terms of their executive roles within the practice. This should relate to important decision making areas, i.e. engagement and dismissal of staff, allocations of workload etc.

In any business responsibilities such as finance, marketing, work allocation and personnel have to be delegated to a responsible person. These executive tasks are solely in the hands of the partners. They must agree on the best style of management which suits them at the time of signing the agreement. This clause will be changed from time to time as the practice develops.

(14) Any prohibitions on partners' activities outside the firm's normal area of work should be detailed.

This particular point must be reviewed regularly as the practice develops. If the partnership is successful, partners are likely to be offered non-executive directorships of companies in property or building-related activities. They may take on arbitrations or be appointed to hospital or governing boards, all of which could have demands on partners' normal working time. Voluntary service spent on institutes, councils, working parties, special delegations etc. can be very time-consuming and can even take over to the detriment of the practice. These honorary tasks seem to creep up on one as time goes by and it is vital to review one's commitment annually and if necessary resign from something to maintain a balance.

Many practices have a policy of appointing a partner in a representative role to the RIBA Council or other special committees. A decision of this nature must be made with great care however, because it takes many years of attendance before one can get to a position of influence in institutional offices and the partner could very easily get out of touch with day to day practice.

(15) Length of holidays or any other staff conditions should be defined in the deed.

Older partners seem to want more holidays for rest and recuperation and younger partners want more time with their families. Staff holidays seem to get longer despite recessions. On the other hand there are partners who are workaholics and take no holidays, working overtime every day and sometimes at weekends. If people work hard they need a rest and should be required to take their full allowance of holidays.

The partners should keep to their agreement and set an example to others. I do not think that sick leave should ever be part of a partnership agreement. It breeds the wrong attitude to health and work.

Partners may have the privilege of longer holidays than the staff but these should not be excessive, and other privileges relating to attendance at conferences, training courses, golf days, cricket days etc. are usually best excluded from the agreement and left to the commonsense of the partners.

(16) Arrangements should be made as to the retirement age of partners.

Some partners want to retire at 55 whilst others prefer to die at the drawing board. This is a decision to be based on personal attitudes. Subject to agreement it is probably better to adhere to the national retirement ages of 60 for women and 65 for men unless there is a strong case put forward by one of the partners, when special provision can be made.

(17) The means by which the partnership will cease should be specified. This will lay down the period of notice to be given by a partner who wishes to withdraw from the partnership or retire, how the assets will be divided, and how work in hand is to be continued if the retiring partner wishes to take more on with some of the ongoing projects.

This is a provision on which you will need advice from your solicitor, accountant and insurance broker, and even perhaps an independent arbitrator. You will need to put aside plenty of time to get this provision right for all partners. There are standard clauses available and they should be carefully scrutinised and adapted for your particular case.

You cannot cover everything in this provision because time and circumstances will create changes anyway. Define as much as you can, the more you have in writing the less you will pay later in fees to solicitors.

(18) The rights of partners should be defined, particularly in relation to their assets on death, bankruptcy, long illness or any misconduct. There should also be provisions for the widow of a deceased partner.

Here again there are some well tried standard clauses available and your solicitor and accountant will advise you. However if there is a wide range of ages in the partnership then far more provisions must be put in than, say, for two young persons at the beginning of a practice. In the latter case it would be well to review this clause, say every five years.

There are insurances available to cover the remaining partners' obligations under these provisions. They are expensive but worth considering. Some spouses of dead partners could have a very expensive life style with plenty of dependants also.

(19) In the event of a partner being disqualified from practice, the deed must define what action can be taken by the partners.

This is not such a great threat these days. The codes of practice of ARCUK and the professional bodies have been amended and the number of cases for breach of the code have diminished. What is more, I know of a practitioner who was disqualified in unlucky circumstances and who told me his practice doubled in size during his disqualification.

The action to be taken should be stated in the agreement and should not be too severe if it is just a minor breach. But if the act has a strategic effect on the practice, there should be a clause to cover such an extreme event which can allow for the dissolution of the partnership.

(20) Provision should be made for arbitration or other means of settling disputes.

Always have this clause clearly defined. Do not name an arbitrator; leave it to the decision of the President of either the RIBA or the Chartered Institute of Arbitrators. They have registers of appropriate independent and experienced persons.

(21) Methods of repayment of capital should be specified.

This provision is really subject to the advice of your accountant whose decision should be final.

(22) The question of indemnifying outgoing partners in the event of a claim for negligence must be defined.

Outgoing and retired partners should be included in your annual indemnity insurance policy.

(23) Terms on which the partnership agreement can be altered should be specified.

The partners should devote time and discussion to this deed because it is fundamental to the nature of their business and a bad deed can cause endless problems and waste of time and money at a future date.

However successful you are in drawing up a near perfect partnership agreement, it will be worthless if the partners do not understand the fundamental basis of partnership which is the compatibility of the partners, their trust and faith in each other and their willingness to make sacrifices for the common good of the practice.

COMPANIES

A company is a quite different vehicle of operation from a partnership. A partnership is never more than the sum total of the individual partners, who are all personally liable for the debts and obligations of the partnership to the full extent of their own property and assets.

By contrast a company has a separate identity quite distinct from the shareholders who comprise it. In lawyer's language, it is a *persona* just like an individual person. It continues to exist whatever changes there are in the shareholders or directors.

A company can be a limited liability one, in which event the shareholders who have paid in full for the nominal value of their shares have no further liability for the debts or other obligations of the company. In normal circumstances, the directors have no personal liability either, although increasingly statutes, such as the Companies Act 1985, the Insolvency Act 1985 and the Company Securities (Insider Dealing) Act 1985, have imposed personal liability in specified circumstances, as has the common law in some situations where the courts have held that a partnership can subsist between the directors of a company and the company itself.

If a company is registered under the Companies Act 1985 with limited liability, it may be either a public limited company (PLC) or a private limited liability company. In the first case, it must include the words or letters 'PLC' at the end of its name and it must have a nominal capital of not less than £50,000. The certificate of incorporation will indicate that it is a public limited company.

Architects' practices have always been allowed to trade as limited liability companies and there is specific provision in the Architects Registration Acts for circumstances in which such companies can use the description 'Architects'. But both the RIBA and ARCUK until recently discouraged this. However, now that the position is accepted, it may well be that a number of large and successful architects' practices will turn themselves into public limited companies and come to either the unlisted securities market or the Stock Exchange. In that way the former partners will be able to capitalise on their success and raise capital for further expansion.

All companies other than public limited companies are private companies. Those that have limited liability for shareholders must include the fact in their title with the accepted and usual abbreviation 'Ltd'.

In recent years, a number of businesses have specialised in selling 'off-the-peg' companies, ready made for little more than £100, and the same businesses will form companies to order for even less. In most cases, it is a waste of time going to a solicitor or accountant to form a company, since these will invariably go to one of these specialists and then treble their fee. The businesses concerned advertise every week in the *New Law Journal* and *Solicitors' Journal*.

In addition to limited liability companies, there are also companies with unlimited liability. These currently seem to be favoured by architects.

An unlimited company is, like a limited one, a separate *persona* distinct from the members who comprise it. However, in the event of a winding-up, the members are liable to contribute to the full extent of the company's debts. The advantages of an unlimited liability company over a limited liability one are:

— No stamp duty is payable on the amounts paid or value of assets contributed to the company on its formation or on any shares paid up in cash. There is, in fact, no obligation on an unlimited company to have a share capital.
— The unlimited company can alter its share capital at any time, simply by passing a special resolution, whereas a limited liability company has a much more involved procedure, including obtaining the permission of the court to reduce capital.
— If the articles of the unlimited company authorise it to do so, an unlimited company can at any time purchase its own shares with its own assets.
— The unlimited company does not have to make a return of allotment of shares to the Registrar of Companies.
— It does not have to deliver copies of its annual accounts to the Registrar of Companies.

— Finally, the unlimited liability status is calculated to inspire confidence in clients.

For any company, a minimum of two persons is necessary. These can constitute the director and secretary. Every company must have at least one director and one secretary, who can also be a director.

The budget of 1984 reduced corporation tax for small companies with profits less than £100,000 per annum to 30 per cent.

Partnerships however, with all their disadvantages from the taxation viewpoint, have had a recent change in NI contributions for self-employed, allowing 50 per cent to be deducted from tax.

The difference for the individual partner or director is the option between the manner in which their personal income is assessed. A partner is taxed on his share of the assessable profits, whether they are drawn or not, but a director will be assessed on PAYE on what he actually receives.

ADVANTAGES AND DISADVANTAGES OF COMPANIES AND PARTNERSHIPS

(1) *Company*
Movement of directors into and out of the company possible without changing the company's name or identity.

Partnership
If a partner dies or leaves the partnership, the partnership agreement is dissolved and a new agreement must be drawn up to allow for the changes.

(2) *Company*
Work in progress is not included in annual accounts. Stock relief possible in annual accounts.

Partnership
Work in progress must be calculated and included in accounts before actual fees are received. Individual partners are taxed on their share of profits.

(3) *Company*
By paying PAYE, at a relatively low rate, directors pay tax at

the time their salary is paid, leaving a much smaller tax bill for higher rates of tax some year or so later.

Partnership
Under Schedule D of the tax laws a partner pays tax on the share of profits of the firm usually in two instalments in January and July, approximately 18 months after the end of the accounting year. This high amount of tax in two instalments can cause hardship.

(4) *Company*
Pensions are easier to administer and decisions regarding the amount to be put aside from income are controlled by the directors. They can have a self-administered scheme which gives greater flexibility in the control of pension sums invested.

Partnership
There are tax advantages offered for partners' pensions but they are for individual decision. Pensions are usually inflexibly invested through insurance companies who have special schemes for businesses. There is the advantage of some tax relief on NI contributions since the 1985 budget.

(5) *Company*
Bank borrowing is usually easier through a company since bank managers understand companies better. However there are some snags, particularly when a company's policy is not to make profits but to reinvest. This means there is not a confidence-building regular profit against capital employed.

Partnership
Banks see large profits from partnerships because partners' income is included in the accounts as profits. They therefore see a larger surplus in the accounts which creates an air of confidence not necessarily backed up by hard cash.

(6) *Company*
Objectives of a company are more restricted than in a partnership.

Partnership
Partnerships are not restricted in choice of operations.

(7) *Company*

If you have young, ambitious architects who are seeking more responsibility you can make them non-shareholding directors, giving them status and opportunities to build up their own clientele with the reward of shareholding if successful.

Partnership

It is difficult to give young, ambitious architects status because you cannot make them partners without affecting the other partners' shareholding and requiring a new partnership agreement. Partnerships can lose good staff because they cannot satisfy the high flyer.

Having been senior partner in two partnerships, once with a majority shareholding, and once with the highest number of shares but not a majority, I believe it does not matter how many shares you hold from the point of view of power and democratic decision making as long as there is a system of consultative management. Even with a majority most people would want to have their partners with them and not against them in the strategic decisions made about the practice's business.

Sometimes a little benevolent dictatorship helps a practice to make tough decisions at the right time to everyone's benefit. A practice without a majority may find itself faced with endless debates and no decisions or with merely a watered down compromise. A voting system for partners' meetings can produce discord in the practice. If decisions are not unanimous, the losing party may well feel hurt or resentful. If this happens regularly he is likely to leave.

In a company where one person has a majority it is solely up to that person to set the style of company management, the working and social environment. If this style can be agreed by the others then success is possible. If not, someone leaves.

Unity of objectives and the procedures to attain these must be the underlying motivation of all in partnerships and companies. Power struggles and differing financial aspirations of members can be controlled if shared endeavour for the good of all is the prime desire of the principals. Many debates relate to design objectives versus profit bottom lines. It should be quite possible to achieve both.

One of the biggest problems facing any small or medium sized practice is raising capital. Any principal in practice who has approached his clearing bank, merchant bank, investors in industry, or insurance company will soon discover that there is a reluctance to lend money to architectural practices. Money can be made available if a certain amount of equity is given up and the lenders have a representative on your board of directors but architectural practice does not easily fit into a banker's concept of a sound investment. The business is too volatile and guarantees can only be obtained from individuals who have very limited assets, many of which could not be liquidated if the bank wanted to recover its money when the firm was in financial difficulties.

However, in June 1985 First Architecture, a London based planning, architecture and interior design firm, became a public limited company. It offered 625,000 shares, priced at 27p, on the over the counter securities market (OTC) and was well over-subscribed. The public investors subscribed a total of £168,750 for 7.14 per cent of the issued share capital at the expense of £54,188 to cover the cost of placing. An advance of £81,250.00 was to be utilized as the general working capital of the group, and the company therefore ended up with finance which was not on loan, nor were the directors mortgaged up to the hilt.

The process of becoming a public limited company

First the architect must contact a dealing company who specialises in placing companies on the market. The dealing company will then organise an investigation of your company to see that it is fit to become a PLC. If they are satisfied, a brochure is then prepared for the purpose of placing and offering the shares at the agreed price. The brochure will deal with the following

(1) History of the business
(2) The market in which it will operate
(3) The management staff

(4) How the firm will operate
(5) The type of clients they already have and expect to get
(6) The forecast for the future
(7) Financial information
(8) Past performance in terms of profit and turnover
(9) The accountant's report
(10) Present cash resources and indebtedness
(11) The use of the proceeds of the placing
(12) Profit projections
(13) The statement on working capital, dividends and the risk factor involved in investment in the company
(14) Prospects for the future
(15) Details of the placing
(16) The company's share capital
(17) The placing price
(18) The definition of over the counter market for this type of company placing
(19) The market for the shares
(20) Method of financial reporting

Additionally information would be given about:

— directors' responsibilities
— constitution in the share capital
— background of the business
— directors' and others' interests and special professional requirements related to directors and the running of the company
— the arrangements with the placing company for fees and management expenses
— details of directors' service contracts with the company
— the articles of association of the company.

Interested parties will also be able to see a list of documents for inspection. All this information has to be provided by the company under the leadership and direction of the placing company. A brochure is prepared and then an announcement is made and the brochures are circulated and sent to those interested. On the appointed day all offers for shares are received and if the application is over-subscribed the company has been successfully launched.

Summary

It is too early to see the effect of this step into the public company field. The directors of the company are working for their shareholders who will expect to see improving dividends and a rise in capital value annually. The directors will earn their salaries and get dividends if the company make good profits. They are open to the usual risks of the stock market and they could be involved in mergers and take-overs. Provided registered architects remain responsible for the design work, this will not present problems. If successful, it offers the continuity of capital resources which is vital for survival in the competitive field of architecture.

THE ROLE OF THE LEGAL ADVISOR

Unless it is very small an architectural practice cannot avoid the cost of employing legal services. Your choice of solicitor can be crucial for anything which legally affects your practice but you may not be able to find a firm of solicitors who have the expertise to carry out the range of legal services you may need. It is not advisable to use just one solicitor for all legal matters, however highly you regard his ability. There is a high degree of specialisation in the legal profession and if you want the best service you have to choose those who have proven track records in the particular service you require.

My practice uses different solicitors for the following:

— General legal advice
— Leases and property
— Planning law
— Professional indemnity claims and fee claims
— Company and partnership law
— Arbitration advice
— Taxation law
— Overseas companies.

All the solicitors have been appointed by recommendation and by making enquiries before a decision was made. Architects get to know clients' solicitors who may well have the special expertise you require and you can sometimes find a good solicitor through this source.

Solicitors' fees are difficult to control. They may quote a fee and time charge at the beginning of a commission but if, say, barristers or experts have to be consulted the cost can radically change.

Never allow solicitors to conduct negotiations for you unless you are present. Make every effort to avoid going to court even if you have to pay the other side more or accept slightly less than you want. Don't do things on principle. It can be very costly, and remember that the only people who profit from the law and its processes are the legal professionals. Costs awarded by courts never cover the real costs for either party. The cost of emotional energy and anxiety can be even more damaging and the loss of time can be highly detrimental to your practice.

5 Administration

Architects like to be involved in project management, designing, solving detail problems or meeting contractors. But most architects do not seem to like involvement in administration. This lack of interest in administration can cause considerable difficulties with lost files, unanswered telephone calls and messages, materials running out when needed. Contracts are lost, petty cash vanishes, fees are not received at the correct time. However boring administration may be to the architect, it is an essential part of the practice and to neglect its importance can prove fatal.

It therefore deserves considerable attention and must be an integrated part of the practice as a whole.

The duties of administration are normally delegated to the senior secretary in small and medium sized practices, or to an office manager in larger practices. It is only when you try to analyse what has to be done in an office that you realise how extensive the duties of an administrator in an architect's office are. Administration is a service to the whole office, and although the administrator is not responsible for the main product of the office, his/her assistance throughout the operation in a supportive role is essential to proper management.

Administrators interpret the office's philosophies, objectives, policies and criteria for evaluating management performance. They prescribe the management controls which are designed to measure performance and reach desired results. They are involved in forecasting the workload of the office, assessing trends in significant areas, identifying where problems can arise and acting to meet those problems at an early stage.

With the assistance of partners or directors they help in drawing up the structure of the organisation, recommending staff and managing the appointment of staff to fill vacancies. They assist in the assignment of authority, responsibility and accountability to the people and teams in the organisation.

In collaboration with book-keepers and accountants they draw up budgets, schedules and standards governing the overall administration of financial matters relating to the practice. They initiate improvements within the office and its organisation when needed. They are responsible for communications throughout the practice so that everybody is appropriately informed. They manage the senior staff's appraisal system of subordinates and they follow through decisions to ensure that the desired results are achieved. They ensure that information and information technology are available to all technical staff and maintain it as a continuing service. They assist the principals in interpreting staff attitudes and maintaining high morale and objectivity throughout the office.

Those people concerned with administration should take on all the tasks which can support those engaged on the technical work. This service frees them from time wasting on chores which other people can do. In order to understand the valuable contribution which administration makes to an office we will now go through the various areas of responsibility which it covers:

— Communications
— External relations
— Internal relations
— Meetings
— Staff administration
— Programming
— Day to day accounting
— Equipment
— Libraries
— The business of information technology
— Materials.

The most demanding of duties imposed on any office administrator is to avoid waste.

COMMUNICATIONS

Post

Every day post comes into the office. It has to be sorted, date stamped and distributed. There has to be a record of deliveries and each office must decide whether the post must be seen by partners or directors before arriving at the desks of job architects and assistants.

The most important principle is that the post should get to the hands of the person who needs to deal with it on the day of its arrival. If partners/directors insist that post must first be seen by them and they are absent for a day or so, this could lead to inefficiencies in the office with frustrated assistants being blamed for the delay. Administrators therefore may have the duty of deciding which post is important and must get to its intended destination quickly, ensuring that the director knows what has been passed on.

The management of post which is leaving the office also requires attention to ensure that it leaves on time, is properly stamped or is delivered to the post office for recorded delivery etc. Matters of this nature can have important consequences, particularly at times when there are disputes or projects are working to very tight time schedules.

Because the post can be unreliable most offices have to make arrangements for special deliveries by taxi or motor cycle where Fax is not available. A proper record must be kept of such deliveries because they are expensive and are sometimes challenged by clients when accounts are rendered.

Internal systems

Internal systems of communication are effected either by an intercom system, telephone system, memos or face to face informal meetings. Whichever is chosen as the best means of achieving internal communication, the administration's duty is to see that the system works well and that people do not experience delays or misunderstandings through lack of a proper system.

EXTERNAL RELATIONS

It is the duty of the administration to set up a good sensible system for dealing with incoming telephone calls and visitors to the office. First impressions are often the longest lasting, and the telephonist's behaviour is the first impression a person will receive when trying to contact your firm. The qualities needed are really quite obvious — clear speech, an easy friendly manner, intelligent reactions to requests and common sense in dealing with them, a continuing climate of efficiency and consideration of the caller's need.

When someone calls at the office either for an appointment, or on the off chance of seeing somebody, the relationship should be more direct and personal. The receptionist should be able to put visitors at their ease, making sure they are comfortable if they have to wait, and provide them with refreshments if necessary.

The reception environment

Callers should be received in a well designed reception area which does credit to the firm and reflects the practice's strength and success.

In small practices this particular activity may be delegated to the secretary/receptionist/book-keeper/general factotum, as there is nobody else to do the job. This person must have considerable qualities, good appearance, charm, friendliness, and a wish to please callers must be paramount.

A medium size firm will normally have a telephonist/receptionist who is situated in the entrance hall. A decision must be made whether she is in her own office with a separate waiting room, so that callers cannot overhear phone conversations, or whether it is better to have her in the same room as the callers.

In large firms where the reception facility is isolated from the telephone serious thought must be given to the effects of both these services on callers to the office.

Receptionists working for large companies may well be placed in a vast entrance hall behind a formal desk with a considerable amount of electronic gadgetry around, visitors' books etc. This tends to make the reception of callers a much more formal event. Very often there is a second receptionist in the actual department to which you are directed and perhaps a further receptionist, the secretary of the person you are visiting.

If this procedure can be carried out smoothly, efficiently and in a friendly manner, then it can be successful. If it is too brusque and formal, a visitor may well feel uncomfortable and uncertain that he will actually reach his destination. This does not give a good impression, and it is an important task of large companies to try to keep the human touch despite their size.

MEETINGS

'Meetings, bloody meetings — why don't they make their own decisions and not rope everyone into make them collectively when they are avoiding the responsibility of making the decisions themselves.' We have all heard people say this. Meetings are the most costly form of communication there is.

Meetings, however, are essential to good co-ordination. Everyone performing management roles must be faced with the decision of whether to have a meeting or not. So let us accept the inevitable — meetings are necessary. There are various types of meetings which can be called in the normal running of an architectural business. It is important first to classify the types of meetings which we need to attend.

Internal meetings

- Board or partners meetings
- Associates or senior executive meetings
- Staff meetings
- Project meetings to cover information, progress, development, problem solving, attitude airing.

External meetings

Architects have to attend a range of meetings with town planning departments, local authority officers' committees and council committees, with building inspectors, fire officers, district surveyors and, of course, with clients.

All take up time, and time is money. Time for travelling, time

Example of costs for meetings
Site meeting in provincial town 100 miles from London:

Attending	Means of travel	Travel hours return	Meeting	Site inspection	Total hours
Client	Car	4	2	1	7
Architect	Car	4	2	1	7
Site engineer	Car	3	2	½	5½
QS	Train/ taxi	5	2	—	7
Service engineer	Car	4	2	—	6
Building contracts manager	Car	2	2	1	5
Site foreman	—	—	2	1	3

Typical cost of a site meeting

Costs:	Travel	Time	Expenditure	Total cost
Client	200 at 40p = £80.00	7 at £80 = £560	£3	£643.00
Architect	200 at 35p = £70.00	7 at £60 = £420	£2	£492.00
Site engineer	150 at 35p = £52.50	5½ at £60 = £330	£2	£384.50
QS	£25 train/taxi	7 at £50 = £350	£10	£385.00
Service engineer	200 at 35p = £70.00	6 at £50 = £300	£2	£372.00
Builder	100 at 40p = £40.00	5 at £60 = £300	£70	£410.00
Site foreman		3 at £40 = £120	£8	£128.00
			Total:	£2 814.50

waiting, time listening to others, time speaking yourself, and time discussing the outcome of the meeting with colleagues who are concerned with the decisions made and preparing minutes of the decisions made at the meeting. The numbers attending meetings must be strictly controlled.

The example on page 73 gives some indication of how much it costs per person per meeting.

Ground rules for meetings

It is therefore important, for the sake of good economy, that the ground rules for meetings are laid down:

(1) They must have a clearly defined purpose.
(2) The objectives to be achieved in the meeting should be stated clearly, so that everyone attending knows exactly why they are there.
(3) Those attending should have the authority to make the decisions necessary at the meeting, without having to refer back to their respective seniors.
(4) The expected length of time to be given to the meeting should be stated and the time objectives should be declared in order that busy people can use their time effectively for other activities on that day. There is nothing worse than to go to a meeting not knowing what you are supposed to do nor how long you will be there. If the meeting is in the morning, you may find yourself cancelling afternoon appointments.
(5) An agenda should be drawn up by the person calling the meeting and should be circulated at least a few days before, so that those attending can come fully prepared.

Let us now look at a list of likely meetings and decide why they are necessary and what matters need to be considered and decided by the meeting.

Partners' or directors' meetings

These meetings are normally held monthly and attended by the most senior members of the office who are normally the partners or the directors, both shareholding or appointed.

Objectives

The objective of these meetings is to see that the firm is being well run, to review what has happened in the past month, to assess the current situation and to make decisions for the future. A typical agenda might be:

Meeting of the directors of . . . .
on Tuesday 13th August 1986

Agenda
(1) Previous minutes
(2) Finance
(3) Fees
(4) Job costs
(5) Programme and workload
(6) Staff
(7) Administration
(8) Marketing
(9) Other business: Charities supported
                           Car changes
                           Personal staff loan
                           Building repairs

Duration of meetings

The length of time taken by these meetings will obviously vary with the size of the firm and the problems to be dealt with. It is suggested that a normal starting time of 10.30 is appropriate, enabling directors to deal with the morning post and to give directions to staff or make important phone calls.

The meeting can go on until lunch time, resume at 2.00 and finish at 4.30. If the meetings are any longer than this, people will become weary, decision making will become slower and probably less effective. If the length of time for the meeting can be reduced to the morning only, so much the better.

Subsequent meetings

Directors' meetings may be followed by meetings with associates or senior executives in order to convey decisions made by the directors and to discuss implementation throughout the firm with those who are responsible for the day-to-day task of putting directors' decisions into action.

Communication of decisions

The remaining members of the staff in turn must be informed, and it is for the executives to decide on the means of communication with staff members. The simplest way is person to person, face to face, but there are times when the whole staff may need to be brought together for meetings.

Staff meetings must also be structured with objectives and agendas for they are an expensive activity without measurable result. Time must be allowed for general discussion, particularly if the meeting is aimed at discussing attitudes. It would be a psychological blunder to prevent staff who perhaps have been waiting many weeks from expressing their feelings about matters affecting the office and which they think are important.

Regular staff meetings are generally very good for staff morale and give them an insight into the running of the whole firm and an appreciation of their particular role in the firm's product. Time and money spent on general staff meetings can often be rewarded in the immeasurable elements of understanding, good morale and enthusiasm.

Information meetings

These meetings are usually conducted between clients, architects and their consultants, between architects, their consultants or specialist sub-contractors, or between architects and general contractors. The objective is to receive instructions and information on which to take action.

Instructions and information require confirmation either in the form of minutes or by exchange of letters, or perhaps the drawing up of the contract, or schedules of instructions confirming a brief which could be short or very long. In fact some hospital authorities may present a whole book as a brief for a building.

It is only by keeping good records of the meetings, particularly detailed client requirements, that information meetings are successful. Often these minutes and schedules become the architect's check list throughout the remaining phases of a project and help to monitor progress.

Development meetings

These meetings are basically for co-ordination. Their objective is to maintain the harmony of the whole operation and to tie up loose ends. These are often attended by a large number of people and it is important to make sure that they do not waste time. It is sometimes a good idea to phase the meeting in such a way that those people making the minimum contribution can leave early and others can come later.

This allows the others who are more concerned with the strategy of the project to concentrate on their work, without having people sitting around the table who are bored and waiting to leave. These meetings should also include any matters dealing with cost evaluation of the project. It is not usually necessary to have meetings where cost only is discussed.

Progress meetings

These are primarily concerned with ensuring that completion of the main objective and other sub-objectives will be in time, in accordance with programmes laid down and yardsticks set at an early stage in the project. Pre-contract meetings are normally held either in the client's or the architect's office, and post-contract on site. The management of time requires considerable skills and a realistic approach to what will actually happen in the future. The building industry generally suffers from the disease of optimism on programming which tends to lead to frustration and irritation in clients when all the assurances of early completion are broken.

Design meetings

Many offices have design meetings, where discussions on design philosophy or actual designs take place. The success of these meetings is very dependent on the attitudes of those attending and their willingness to accept criticism, and the general avoidance of destructive criticism made for personal reasons. They can be very effective in unifying the firm's design strategy and detailed design policy, but they may require very skilful handling by the chairman to retain objectivity.

Staff account for 50 to 70 per cent of all the costs of running an architectural business. There are basically two types of staff, technical and administrative. The efficiency of the firm can often be measured in terms of the number of administrative to technical staff. Depending on the size of the firm, the ratio can be anything from 1:3 to 1:6. It is the duty of the principals of a firm to see that this expensive resource is fully employed and efficient, producing the maximum profitable work. This implies that people should be of the highest quality, with the competence to do the job to which they are assigned.

The policy should be to give rewards related to responsibility and to aim at personal satisfaction and fulfilment. The ways of achieving these objectives are many and varied. Let us look at the methods by which staff are recruited, graded, employed, and their enthusiasm maintained to the enhancement of overall office morale.

Staffing the small office

When I started in practice, I had recently married, moved into a flat, and the spare bedroom was designated the new architect's office. It was big enough for a drawing board and a desk with a telephone. There were no plan chests or storage files because no work had yet been obtained. But within a few weeks, the office began to pile up with paper, the telephone was in frequent use, I needed to write letters, be away at meetings, prepare drawings, get them printed and posted off. I had to keep records of transactions and do the books. In fact I had to do everything including typing one or two letters on a very old tired typewriter.

It did not take me very long to realise that some of my skilled time was being wasted on very menial chores. I did not always like working by myself and I missed the social relationships of my previous office. I also found very soon that people who wished to contact me by telephone became frustrated because I could not answer when I was out on site or at local authority offices.

Consequently within five months, I decided that this was not the best way to practise and I therefore joined others in founding a shared facilities group practice, which could give me an economic administrative base, and enable me to share out the work over the peaks and troughs of architectural practice, and have time to expand through meeting people.

It is still true to say that there are many architects who practise on their own but the majority (approximately 80 per cent) practise in very small offices or in their own house with a staff of up to 10 people.

The first thing you discover when starting up in practice on your own is that projects are normally small, usually paid for by persons who are paying out money from their own pocket, and however well you plan to receive fees, they are usually paid late and what is more the client is often seeking to reduce the payment.

In this type of climate, if you find you have too much work to handle by yourself, then the choice is either to get other architects to ghost for you, or to employ staff.

The first assistant

The first person normally required is an assistant to carry out drawings and reduce the amount of time the principal spends at the drawing board, because this is the most time consuming activity.

If you want to get rid of the chores, it is then a matter of employing a part time secretary. A part time secretary and a junior assistant need proper accommodation and, if you started off in your home to save costs, it soon becomes apparent it is better to find an office away from your home or build one in the back garden if space allows.

The need for administration

As soon as you employ staff and move into leased premises, your administration increases. The telephone needs answering all day, you need full time administrative assistance. This administrative assistant will be a person who takes letters, does the elementary book-keeping, and answers the telephone as a receptionist — a 'mini' office manager.

The junior assistant is normally employed on the lowest salary possible, in order to reduce costs which are always a strain on a small office. Very often, the junior assistants will be students or part time day students who cannot take complicated instructions, need constant supervision and are not capable of dealing with the management of projects on their own.

Growing pains
Despite these difficulties, if the workload increases, you may well find yourself with a small but growing practice of three assistants, one of whom will be a senior, perhaps recently qualified, architect, and a secretary/general factotum. This description probably covers the majority of small practices in Great Britain.

The principal may want to keep his practice at that size, as an easily managed unit. He may then work something like 70 hours a week, with his staff probably working just a little less, and with a secretary who does not mind staying late when the heat is on. This organisation is a happy family working at minimum cost on small projects where, because of their nature, the architect has to put in considerable organisational work to control disorganised small builders.

Usually most of the work is in the locality and therefore the staff can get to sites using public transport. A senior assistant may have his own car on expenses, the business car being run by the principal. Sometimes the wife may act as the secretary/office manager, which can be a very successful partnership, but not necessarily beneficial to their offspring. Either way the principal will need an understanding spouse.

Selecting staff for the small office
Selecting staff for such a small practice means often having to decide on the employment of somebody who may carry out 25 per cent of all your work. Therefore the choice and quality of the person will be crucial to the success of the practice as a whole. Personality will be as important as technical competence because of the close working relationships in a small office.

The medium sized practice of 10–25 people

It requires considerable effort to move from a practice of five to 10 persons to a small organisation with partners or associates, a hefty wage bill every month, ever increasing overheads and a larger number of clients from more substantial organisations. The principal who has become accustomed to being the centre of everything, making all the decisions, and being intensely busy in and out of the office, finds that his working style must change radically.

Delegation — a tough discipline

The first and most important thing is to learn something about management and particularly delegation. It is true to say that whenever you expand any form of business you will have more interesting and different challenges, but will have to sacrifice those things which were once enjoyable.

The first sacrifice is probably that you will have to share the practice with others, equal or subordinate, who will expect to share in the decision making process. You will no longer have a direct relationship with all the clients, as there are probably too many for you to spare the time to see them all. They will have to be handled by other senior people in your office.

You are likely to see the post nearly every day and be involved in the engagement of staff, but you will probably already have delegated the engagement of junior administrative staff to one of your partners or co-directors. Therefore, the directors and partners have to choose what they will do for the benefit of the practice as a whole. They will have to capitalise on their special expertise and share responsibilities.

Some staff will join the firm for full time career opportunities, while others will come and go as birds of passage. The administrative staff may have grown around the original secretary, who may now become the office administrator and senior partner's secretary, or perhaps could not cope with change and left to go to another small practice.

All other functions are delegated. There may still be a family atmosphere but a structure for the firm will begin to be needed.

Structure

It is necessary to have a structure in order to define clearly how the hierarchy works, what functions go on in the office, and who will carry them out. It should distinguish between administrative staff and technical staff and show how delegation is effected throughout the office.

The staff should know of this structure and their position in it, and clearly made decisions will result in clearly defined duties for the whole staff. The senior people in the firm will have to put more time into organising staff in addition to the time they will spend with clients, and it is therefore likely that their time will be broken up with a variety of activities each day.

The three main executive levels in the structure are:

— directors/partners
— associates
— job architects.

Each has to maintain a variety of contacts and relationships as the following diagrams show.

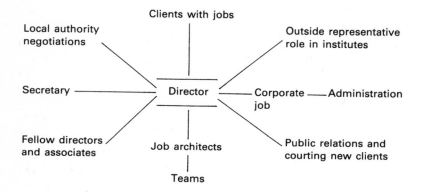

The director or partner is the top management of a practice and has many roles and relationships in his span of work. From day to day all the above contacts may be made. They require a careful control of time to be spent on many activities and an overall balance in the individual's attitude to the duties which go with his job.

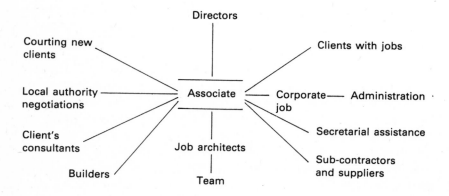

The associate is the middle management with executive responsibilities to see that either a number of smaller jobs or one large job are well run. His main relationships are with job architects, local authority departments, consultants and contractors. He will have a continuing relationship with the client for whom he is running the job. He may be assigned to, or from his own contacts find, new clients to be courted. Within the organisation he will have a corporate job and have continuous contact with the administration.

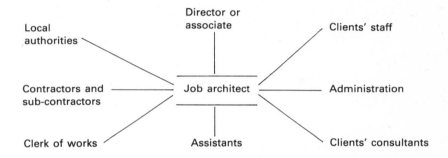

The job architect is the *line* manager who is directly responsible for the product of the office. He has a line relationship with the directors, associates and assistants concerned with his projects. He will use the administration for support and services. Running jobs will bring him into direct contact with contractors, consultants, clerks of works and local government officers. He will deal with clients' staff and take direct instructions. He can be involved in the design, technical process and contract administration of many jobs at once at varying stages of development.

The larger practice — 25+ persons

In the large practice, which is much more structured, there will normally be someone in charge of the appointment of staff, personnel matters and the organisation of resource allocation. For the firm which is expanding to this size there comes a point when the staff gets over about 30, and decisions have to be made as to whether you are going to stay in the same building or decentralise.

In a centralised organisation, the structure begins to have many levels, and this is a danger which must be resisted. There should never be more than four levels of management in an architectural practice, and it is better organised on a three level basis. At the first level will be directors and senior staff, job architects and project managers will form the next, whilst at the third level will be architects and technicians. This is by far the best method of maintaining communication and the transmission of information.

If it is decided to decentralise, the same principles apply but more effort has to be put into communication between the branches to retain the unity of the practice as a whole. In a large practice staff can often see a career ahead of them which will enable them to develop within the organisation.

In large practices there is a greater movement of junior staff and sometimes very large reductions or increases in a short period. Therefore it is difficult to maintain a high standard of morale and systems have to be established in order that staff standards can be maintained in all aspects of the firm's work.

Staff policy

The procedures necessary to employ the best quality staff often change according to market conditions. During boom periods, when there is a shortage of available staff, you may have to offer high salaries or endeavour to meet people who can be enticed from other practices to yours. When you advertise, there may not be any good staff available and you may therefore have to take on staff who are not really up to your standard and who therefore have to be carefully supervised. In these circumstances, the employer must take what is available and accept the quality, but with good training and back-up supervision in the office, these people can sometimes be transformed into useful members of staff.

In periods of slump and recession there is a surplus of good staff, but this brings its own problems. When advertising for staff you normally need not state the salary, you can take your choice and negotiate from a position of strength. There may well be too many applicants and there is then the difficult task of drawing up a shortlist. Nowadays, those applying are sometimes of a higher calibre than the job requires and this creates a dilemma as to whether to employ such people in the hope that business will improve and they can be elevated to their proper level.

In boom periods there are always difficulties with staff claiming rises, wanting to cash in on the expansionist phase. In slumps, salary increases are less of a problem, but there is always an atmosphere of insecurity which has to be allayed so that productivity can be maintained. In slumps there will always be times when many people have to leave at once because a large job has come to an end and there is nothing in the foreseeable future. In these cases you have to select the staff you can afford to see leave and at times it is very difficult to be fair and reasonable in decision making of this nature. When technical staff leave, normally administrative staff also have to be selected for redundancy and this can unbalance the administration and have a detrimental effect on those who are left in the practice. Very seldom can you keep the practice in absolute equilibrium, except in periods of transition between boom and slump. Because architectural business is very volatile, whatever stage you are in there are always problems related to staff.

Resources review

Most practices employ the principle of matching people to the jobs which need to be done, and operate some form of staff appraisal which is related to bonus or profit sharing schemes. All these activities rely on information provided by the administration to partners or directors.

Selection/appointment procedures

The administration normally advises on whether it is best to advertise or go to agencies for staff. Both systems are expensive and if not properly managed can also be time wasting. There are good and bad times to advertise for staff. The bad times are around Christmas and holiday periods in the summer. The good times are usually in between.

First it must be decided what job needs to be done, the title of the job, job specification and salary range. This information is then communicated to the medium in which you wish to advertise or to the agency so that your requirement is clearly understood. The name address and phone number of the person who will administer the job interview procedures should be included. You must decide whether you require phone calls or written submissions with *curricula vitae* from applicants in order to draw up a short list.

When interviews are arranged by telephone calls the administrator must ensure that the interviewing partner or senior staff are available and will have sufficient time for the interview, setting a time limit for the number of interviews required and when a decision must be taken.

In the case of written submissions a final date for submission should be given. Evaluation should be made by the administrator and a partner or director and a short list drawn up. The applicants must be informed, a day selected for the interview and a final date for a decision.

The interviews should be conducted by architects for technical staff, and architects and administrators for clerical staff, so that potential applicants can be fully appraised. There are many books and courses dealing with interviewing techniques and appraisal systems along with many philosophies on how to select the best person for your firm. Interviewing applicants for jobs is a special skill and someone in your organisation should have some training in this field, so that you can maintain and even improve the quality of person coming into your practice.

When the person to be appointed has been selected, the administration must oversee the procedures by which the terms of their employment are properly defined and a contract of employment drawn up. All tax office requirements must be properly administered and, when the person comes to the office a place must have been prepared for them.

Staff must be welcomed on their first day, met by their immediate superior and rapidly integrated into the office staff. New staff must be made aware of the office standards and procedures, methods of working, times of working, and any other administrative duties which could be made available in an office manual.

Staff management

Every member of staff has at some time problems which require attention from the administration. There should be staff records of progress, sickness and holidays on a personal file which is always available for reference. Staff management should look after the staff's development and attendance at courses and training, and expect to be concerned with personal matters related to loans, divorce, death of relatives and family traumas. If the staff feel that management is concerned with their well being and security, then this is a sound foundation for the maintenance of good morale throughout the practice.

Programming and organisation of staff time and costs

The administration is responsible for presenting management information to the partners, directors or committees operating within the practice. They must present budget information on all matters affecting financial decisions and keep records relating to those decisions for comparison purposes. For management accounting operations they will prepare cash flows, planning charts, time and cost job records and analyses. Although administrators may not make decisions on these management aids, it is their responsibility to see that the information is properly collated and presented to the appropriate person or committee for decisions.

Finally, holidays can have an important effect on work programmes during the summer period and it is the administration's duty to gather together all information on staff holidays and to weld this into an effective programme and identify those areas where action is needed.

Management techniques which help to control time

We frequently hear building contractors say optimistically: 'We'll make up time lost and finish on programme.' This is impossible. Time lost is never regained and therefore we should always carefully value time. There is a difference between timing and the control of time. Timing relates to the initiation, change and stopping of action. Time is the measuring of activities over a period defined by a programme to reach goals.

The first management aid needed for the control of time is a linear timetable of all secured projects in the office broken down into the stages of the plan of work and coloured if necessary for quick recognition.

A programme such as the one on page 88 should be a strategic reference for anyone planning work in the office. It should be

TIMETABLE			DATE 3/8/85	No. 4	

| MONTH | | | SEP | | | | OCT | | | | NOV | | | | DEC | | | | JAN | | | | FEB | |

JOB No.	PROJECT TITLE	PROJECT DIRECTOR	1	2	3	4	5	6	7	8	9	10	11	12	13	14	15	16	17	18	19	20	21	22	23	24	25	26
3010	Limpet St	CD	EF										G							H				K				
3012	Highview Gdns	HG	D		D2	TO	APPEAL																					
3017	Park Mews	CD	K																									
3022	Elm Avenue	AF	K							L	M													■				
3026	5-9 Uppers	HG	EF	K																								
3030	Redville Stn.	CD	D																									
3054	Lower Rd	LS	L	M															■									
3059	Pell Mell	LS				EF						G			H							J			K			
3060	Unit 34 A.D.	AF	L								■																	
3061	Windlock Ho.	HG			G							H							J									
3065	Bonte St	AF	M							■																		
3071	Quest Park	CD	K															L	M									
3073	N.W. Plot 6	LS	C					D																				
3076	Wold Way	CD	G							H						J						K						
3078	Dawn Mans.	AF	D								EF																	
3079	N.W. Plot 7	LS					D				APPEAL																	

– by adding different colours to the stages, peaks and troughs can be foreseen at a glance.

– to be updated monthly.

reviewed and adjusted monthly. Each job should have its own job control bar line chart. Critical events such as planning approval and tenders can be emphasised (see page 89). The chart should cover a period of at least one year.

This chart should be appraised monthly and any adjustments entered. Time sheets are essential for proper time and cost control. Ideally they should be filled in at the end of each day but definitely not longer than every week (see page 90).

The other means of communication is a bar line chart with 'float'. This is prepared if a critical path network analysis is to be used for programming. Critical path is only used on large complicated projects. After the job bar line programme is approved and regularly updated it is necessary to break down the staff time to forecast how to meet the programmed targets.

Forecast of time to be spent on a project

Times should be recorded in a time control book or computer and then costed by multiplying the man hour cost. The information

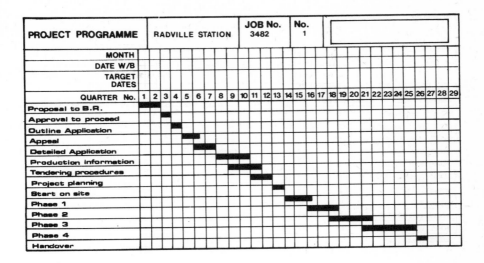

PROJECT PROGRAMME	RADVILLE STATION	JOB No. 3482	No. 1	

	1	2	3	4	5	6	7	8	9	10	11	12	13	14	15	16	17	18	19	20	21	22	23	24	25	26	27	28	29
MONTH																													
DATE W/B																													
TARGET DATES																													
QUARTER No.																													
Proposal to B.R.																													
Approval to proceed																													
Outline Application																													
Appeal																													
Detailed Application																													
Production information																													
Tendering procedures																													
Project planning																													
Start on site																													
Phase 1																													
Phase 2																													
Phase 3																													
Phase 4																													
Handover																													

from the time control book or computer should then be recorded on to a job cost and time chart (see page 91). This shows how much has been spent against the forecast and the actual fee payment and should show the profitability of the project. The dotted lines show the forecast of fee based on monthly payments, the thin line the actual record of costs and the thick line the actual fee income.

The results can be tabulated on a job comparison basis and then related to individual architect's programmes or team performance on the job. It helps you to ask questions and understand what actually happened on each job, and the information gained improves future forecasting and can indicate where remedial action can be taken.

Management techniques which help to control technical staff

Technical staff have to be fully and usefully employed on feasibility projects and ongoing projects. In small offices the former will be done quickly by the principal, but as the office expands in size there could be a feasibility person expanding to a feasibility team. For ongoing projects time allocation comes from programmes. From this information a schedule of work and drawings can be prepared and staff allocated (see top illustration on p. 92). This diagram is a forecast and plan of how jobs will be staffed over a twelve month period.

TIME SHEET

Name	D.Small
W.E.	6/6/85

NON PROJECT

	M	T	W	T	F		TOTAL	SPECIAL COMMENTS
HOLIDAYS								
SICK TIME								
P.R. TIME	2		4		2		8	
ADMIN	1			2			3	
TRAINING								

TOTAL NON PROJECT HOURS   `11`

PROJECTS

JOB No.	JOB NAME	CODE	M	T	W	T	F		TOTAL	SPECIAL COMMENTS
1662	Radville Stn.	2	2						2	Survey instruction
1700	Dawn Park	1			1		3		4	
1556	Hubton St	3A	1			4			5	
1660	Quest Park	2	1	4	1				6	
1444	Lower Rd.	4	2			2			4	
1645	Pell Mell	6			2				2	Fee paid by adj. owner
1670	Bonte St	3		3		1			4	
1650	Wold Mews	2					2		2	

TOTAL PROJECT HOURS   `29`

CODES:

PART 1	NORMAL DUTIES		CODE	R.I.B.A. STAGES
	FEASIBILITY & PLANNING		1	A – D
	DESIGN & PRODUCTION		2	E – H
	SITE SUPERVISION	SITE VISITS	3A	J – L
		IN OFFICE	3B	J – L
	POST COMPLETION		4	M

PART 2	ADDITIONAL DUTIES	CODE
	SURVEY	5
	PARTY WALL AGREEMENTS	6
	FITTING OUT / TENANTS WORK	7
	REDESIGN	8
	PROMOTIONAL /LETTING	9
	OTHERS (Specify)	10

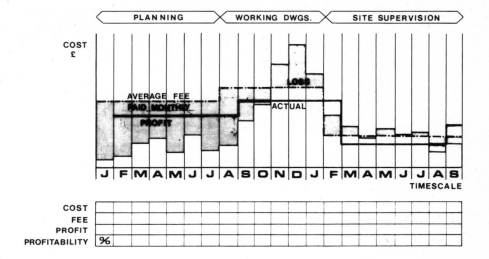

	PLANNING	WORKING DWGS.	SITE SUPERVISION

COST £

AVERAGE FEE
PAID MONTHLY
PROFIT
ACTUAL
LOSS

J	F	M	A	M	J	J	A	S	O	N	D	J	F	M	A	M	J	J	A	S

TIMESCALE

COST																				
FEE																				
PROFIT																				
PROFITABILITY	%																			

JOB MONITORING

OPERATION

- to monitor expenditure levels against income to control the level of job profitability.
- to be monitored at least monthly.
- valuable feedback is gained for the assessment of future fee agreements.

Weekly staff allocation
From a chart, such as the one below on page 92, a weekly allocation sheet can be prepared and used at a weekly Monday morning meeting where the whole staff or a department can get together and ensure that all jobs are covered and staff allocated.

Staff level planning
This information can be put into an annual projection of staff needed in order to plan ahead for strategic staff needs (see example on page 93).

The control of money related to time and staff is described in Chapter 6.

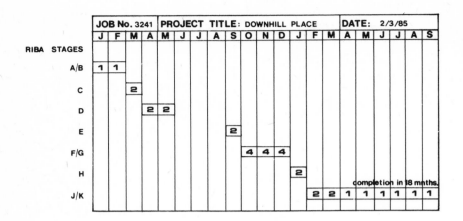

JOB No. 3241	PROJECT TITLE: DOWNHILL PLACE												DATE: 2/3/85						
RIBA STAGES	J	F	M	A	M	J	J	A	S	O	N	D	J	F	M	A	M	J	J	A	S
A/B	1	1																			
C			2																		
D				2	2																
E								2													
F/G									4	4	4										
H												2				completion in 18 mnths.					
J/K													2	2	1	1	1	1	1	1	1

STAFFING JOB PLAN

OPERATION

- to indicate probable staff levels for individual jobs.
- to be updated monthly by job architect in response to programme changes.
- to be used for producing Stategic Staff Plan.

AUGUST

JOB		5	6	7	8	9		12	13	14	15	16
A		AB	AB	AB	AB	–		–	–	AB	–	–
		JR	JR	–	–	–		JR	JR	–	–	–
B		–	–	JR	–	–		–	–	JR	–	–
C		–	–	–	JR	JR		–	–	–	JR	JR
		PC	PC	PC	PC	PC		PC	PC	PC	PC	PC

WEEKLY STAFF ALLOCATION

OPERATION

- to allocate staff on a daily basis over a two week period.
- to ensure adequate staffing levels for all jobs.
- to be updated weekly.

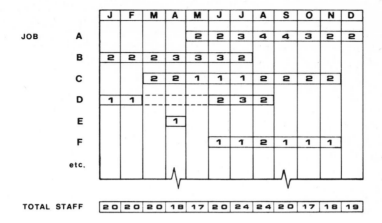

	J	F	M	A	M	J	J	A	S	O	N	D
JOB A					2	2	3	4	4	3	2	2
B	2	2	2	3	3	3	2					
C			2	2	1	1	1	2	2	2	2	
D	1	1				2	3	2				
E				1								
F						1	1	2	1	1	1	
etc.												
TOTAL STAFF	20	20	20	18	17	20	24	24	20	17	18	19

STAFF LEVEL PLANNING

OPERATION
- to forecast staffing levels over a six or twelve month period.
- to predict potential problems arising from lack of work or too few staff.
- to be updated monthly.

DAY TO DAY ACCOUNTING

The financial control and management of the office is described in Chapter 6, but the general duties in relation to finance have to be organised on a day to day, year to year basis by the administration. These duties are usually carried out by a book-keeper or accountant and they are as follows.

Daily

Work done daily includes banking, petty cash, incoming mail and entries into the double entry book-keeping system.

Weekly

Every week petty cash control activities are carried out and there is an update of the situation at the bank.

Monthly

Fee accounts are sent out monthly. Salaries are prepared monthly and despatched. PAYE tax is paid. Month end accounts are settled. Office bills are paid and staff expenses are recorded and paid. These records are analysed. Cash flows are presented to partners/directors meetings. Debit and credit statements are presented. List of fees outstanding and fees expected are also presented. There is also a bank reconciliation and statement drawn up for directors/partners meetings.

Quarterly

On a quarterly basis there is a trial balance which is compared with the annual budget and the last quarterly forecast. There is a disbursements balance and a VAT return to be made.

Annually

Annually there is the annual audit, setting up of new files for the year, and the old year's filing put away, the writing off of all books and the trial balance compared with the annual budget forecast.

From day to day new jobs are set up, cheques are paid, fee accounts are rendered and petty cash is paid. The system is usually drawn up by the practice's chartered accountant and it is the administrator's duty to see that this system is working at all times and is serving the practice adequately.

EQUIPMENT

In collaboration with the principals of the practice decisions are made regarding furniture and fittings and the purchase and maintenance of expensive equipment for long life. It is the task of the administration to see that all these operations are smoothly managed, that contracts, invoices and maintenance arrangements are properly attended to, and that the practice is properly equipped for its task.

Architects' offices are full of furniture and equipment, all of which has to be purchased, maintained and eventually discarded for new office systems. The office policy will be decided by the directorate but the administration will implement and maintain the results of directors' decisions.

One of the first directions must be related to choice of furniture and fittings which are moveable or fixed. Some offices work out a preferred office layout and then provide fixtures which are immoveable. Others prefer total flexibility, all furniture and equipment being moveable. My personal preference is for a totally moveable system. It allows rapid changes to meet revisions in project teams or office rearrangements. A total move around sometimes benefits the whole office and gets rid of fixed habits and territorial cobwebs.

The selection of equipment can be classified into three types:

(1) furniture
(2) electrical and mechanical machines
(3) storage equipment.

(1) **Furniture**

The average architect needs a drawing board, chair, desk, plan chest and storage for immediate references. A secretary needs a desk, chair, table and filing cabinets. Conference rooms need tables, chairs, cupboards and display equipment. Entrance halls need easy chairs, a desk, table and displays.

All furniture can be very cheaply purchased second hand for newly created practices and with discounts for the established practice. The choice should be determined by design image, practicality, flexibility and ease of maintenance.

(2) **Electrical and mechanical machines**

This is the fastest expanding area of office equipment. Much of what is bought today is obsolete in two years and ancient within five.

Equipment would include electronic calculators, typewriters, word processors, accounting machines, franking machines, information retrieving machines, microfiche VDUs, copiers, plotters, communication equipment, telephones which are also intercoms and pagers, facsimile copiers, bleepers and cellnet telephones.

The task of keeping up-to-date and buying the best and most suitable equipment for your operation is a challenging task for the administration. For any major installation such as graphic computers a long period of research and expert advice is needed, for the cost is high and a mistake could be disastrous.

(3) Storage equipment

This is mainly for storage of drawings, files, records and materials.

The office policy for storage of drawings can be variable. The choice lies between traditional horizontal plan chests and vertical suspension. Old drawings are either left in drawers, which is very uneconomic in floor space and storage, put into rolls in a basement store or micro-filmed. I prefer the latter system as it is the safest. Files take up much space, whether you use horizontal drawer filing cabinets or vertical lateral cupboards.

There is a choice of either a centralised filing room or a decentralised system of filing cabinets beside the job architects. I prefer the latter system as it allows the files to be at hand for daily reference.

Old files can be stored in boxes and after six years they can be destroyed. If this is your practice it is advisable to keep the main documents for the sake of your clients or for reference and possible litigation. Alternatively the files can be stored on microfilm which can be very expensive if the files are not edited and reduced. Some files can be stored on computer discs but this could also be expensive and there is always the risk of erasure.

Means of purchase

Depending on the firm's cash position and accountants' advice, the advantages and disadvantages of leasing, hire purchase and outright purchase can be decided.

Outright purchase usually brings with it the advantage of large discounts, but you are using up valuable working capital. Leasing is long term payment but not ownership, and there are tax advantages. With hire purchase there are also tax advantages, you own the equipment in the end but it may be obsolete.

Attention to the management of the purchase, maintenance and disposal of equipment can save the firm money, lead to greater efficiency and avoid waste.

MATERIALS

The selection, ordering and control of materials is another administrative function. Architects use a great variety of materials in their work. It is the job of the administrator to provide the materials, keep stock and advise on new developments. The most important material is paper, which is probably the largest cost item. The control, storage and issuing of materials is best left to one person in the office, who is totally responsible.

INFORMATION NEEDS

As has already been said, architects are in the information business: they collect a variety of information and convert this into building data for communication to consultants, clients, builders and statutory bodies.

Most of our input information is obtained from libraries, usually from our own office source, but there is an additional daily source from papers, journals, reports, commercial circulars, radio and television which broaden our knowledge.

Clients expect their architects to be up-to-date with what is in the news. Every week we receive professional newspapers and journals which keep the architect informed about developments, new products, latest buildings, new standards and codes, exhibitions, conferences etc. Monthly journals deal with business prospects, new building methods and products, practice notes, education news, and government legislation. We have a duty to read these sources of information and follow up those items which have a direct relationship with our practices.

The administration will be responsible for overseeing the library service in your office, either by paying for an outside agency to keep the library up-to-date or by employing a librarian directly.

The office library must have up-to-date catalogues, addresses and details of legislation, all for immediate use. This information should be divided into sections.

(1) *Products*
    Research and development information

Standard products and specifications
Performance data
New products
Prices

(2) *Services*
Professional, particularly consultants' information
Equipment for office
Specialist services for office support

(3) *Legislation*
Green papers, white papers
Acts of Parliament — amendments
Government circulars
Codes of practice, British Standards, European CEN
   Standards,
Building and other regulations
Overseas legislation, if appropriate
General legal information, i.e. property, practice, arbitration

(4) *General information*
Building industry statistics
Economic trends
Company reports
Marketing information

Remember, speed of access is vital, information is most useful if it can be used by comparison. Collecting information for its own sake is wasteful and care must be taken to ensure that the cost of obtaining the information is not more than its value to you.

Information technology

Most of us, when preparing designs or production information, use our own office libraries for technical information, and normally have handbooks on design data which have proved useful. If we want further information we normally telephone companies and arrange for technical representatives to call. If greater detail is required, a specialist sub-contractor may well provide the necessary information to develop the scheme. This is a very time consuming and laborious task, and it is said that many architects spend approximately 25 per cent of their time actually collecting and disseminating information.

Information technology, and the use of computers, are now destined to save considerable time, with the architect being able to call up much information on a screen and have it printed out if he wants to keep it, without moving away from his desk.

Using computers

Information such as cash flows, job budgets and costing, historic records and future projections can all easily be stored and produced on computer once this has been properly programmed and the information has been fed in on a proper disciplined basis. The paper work will then actually increase because it will be so much easier to get together important business and technical information and have it presented in an easily readable and understandable manner. On balance therefore computers offer greater efficiency in the office, less time spent on routine chores, and more effective time on the vital parts of the job which require specialist skills.

The other area which will use computer facilities is draughting. Architects waste considerable time, money and energy in preparation of highly finished, but really unsuitable drawings for builders. Each drawing is carried out to different scales according to depth of information required and everything is produced by hand. This is very labour intensive and painstaking. Most of the drawings are overdeveloped for their particular need and efficient use, largely because the draughtsman feels the need to gain satisfaction from the quality of the drawing. Computer draughting overcomes many of these problems.

First, it imposes a discipline on the architect or technician to work out thoroughly how the building is going to be put together, the information needed for the drawing, and the sequence in which it will be drawn. The information is then put into the computer using the computer screen and is developed into a completed drawing and stored in the memory. Any scale can be produced from the same drawing and then it can be printed. The plotting of even complex drawings, which will take approximately a day to produce, can normally be completed in minutes.

The advantage of this system is obvious and it is fairly certain that every office will have these facilities as long as they can afford to pay the price of installation. The other advantage related to this form of draughting is that information can be stored and used for other projects in an easy manner, rather than the old system of having standard drawings which draughtsmen normally could not be bothered to choose and print, as they would rather draw out the same thing over and over again for each job. The computer stores the information and the draughtsman can call it up without any labour. The detail can then be incorporated in the current project.

Because computer draughting is really the use of machines, the management of these machines becomes very important. As in all industrial processes, it is sensible if you are making a big investment in machinery to make sure the machinery is used intensively during its useful life. Therefore architects with these types of computers, will have to resort to shift systems, decide on the tasks the computer does well and do the rest by hand.

The use of computer systems requires a radical change of attitude by the staff and a patient working-up period to reach optimum effectiveness in the use of the machines. Once through this learning period, the momentum which is gathered, and seen to be effective, is so compelling that the staff are convinced this is the most satisfying and fulfilling way of producing drawing information.

Computers can also be used for design development because of their three dimensional graphic display facilities. The only problem is that in order to use that facility, you have to use expensive equipment for long periods to play with the design. This may not be the most economical way of utilising graphic computers. However, it is particularly effective when designing complex shapes, co-ordinating services or preparing multiple views of the interiors of buildings for clients' approval. Again, these computers will be very common in architects' offices in the not too distant future. Does this mean that the drawing board will become obsolete? I think so. There may be a few drawing boards in offices for doing sketch designs or working-up designs and presentation drawings, but other than that, the advantages of graphic computers are so compelling as to defeat any romantic notions or habits derived from the use of a drawing board.

Facsimile copies (FAX)

To convey a piece of information in drawing form from architect to client or to contractor is a long process. If many changes in the drawing are necessary many weeks could pass. FAX offers the facility of immediate communication, a dialogue, a decision and an agreed drawing confirming the instruction. The transaction can be completed within the same day. The saving in time and the accuracy of communication makes a compelling case for FAX.

SUMMARY ON ADMINISTRATION

As can be clearly seen from the foregoing, administration is a crucial activity in an architect's office. More attention to this area of the practice can bring great time and cost rewards without higher expenditure. The efficient use of resources, the service support to the technical staff and the overall morale of the office is dependent on a good administrative policy. In order to see that this policy is being pursued, there should be an administration meeting at least quarterly. A typical agenda might be as follows:

Admin meeting agenda
(for quarterly meetings)

External Relations
(a) Reception
(b) Telephones
(c) Appearance/Internal area

Communications
(a) External mail
(b) Special deliveries
(c) Internal systems
(d) Meetings
(e) Storage of records

Staff
(a) Resources review
(b) Accommodation
(c) Selection and appointment
    procedures
(d) Staff management

Programming
(a) Forecasts and planning
(b) Budgets
(c) Holidays

Financial
(a) Petty cash
(b) Fees organisation
(c) Contracts
(d) Bank arrangements
(e) Salaries management

Equipment
(a) Furniture and fittings
(b) Drawing office equipment
(c) Printing
(d) Computers

Information
(a) Library and technical information
(b) Graphs, charts for management
(c) Filing and records
(d) Materials
(e) Office manual revisions

Materials
(a) Administrative
(b) Drawing and technical
(c) Storage

6 Financial and management accounting

In order to start up in practice capital is needed and to run a practice working capital must be available. Where can we get this money?

A number of architects have money left to them, or inherit property or assets. These can be used as collateral when borrowing money, and a loan can be provided normally up to three quarters of the value of those assets. The value of the assets has to be proven by independent valuation before the banks will lend. Repayments are normally on a long, medium or short term basis at a rate of interest of about 2½ per cent above the bank base rate. This will vary from time to time according to market conditions.

Loans

If you have no large assets, but have a flow of work, banks will lend money subject to guarantees, to such sums as they think are appropriate to their risk. Insurance companies will also lend money, linked with life policies and pension plans, based on statements and forecasts of income and expenditure. Merchant banks may lend venture capital in special cases at much higher rates of interest than clearing banks, taking an equity interest.

The simplest and best method is to borrow money from a clearing bank, by short, medium or long term loan, or by fixing an overdraft limit and working within it. Both systems can be used at the same time. Often you can get medium or long term loans against a specific cost on the practice, e.g. purchase of property or of a computer installation, and run an overdraft up to a limit acceptable to the bank. You can also go to different banks or have a variety of facilities, as long as you meet the bank's criteria and policies for lending.

Insurance companies normally want very long term loans linked with insurances and usually their interest rates are higher than the clearing banks.

Other sources of business finance

There are many more sources and methods of business finance available today. Listed below are some of the schemes and methods which you can suggest to your accountant and see whether one or more could be of assistance to you:

— Government loan guarantee scheme
— Government business expansion scheme
— Venture capital
— High tech finance
— Clearing bank schemes
— Factoring
— Leasing
— Enterprise allowance scheme
— Enterprise agencies
— Sale and leaseholds
— Government construction grants and development loans
— Unlisted securities market.

MANAGEMENT ACCOUNTING

Management accounting is concerned with providing financial information for forecasting, planning and decision making. There are very many techniques and systems available from which to choose the best for your business. Management accounting relies on information, but we must first understand that information is only of use if it can be compared with something. Figures on their own are meaningless, and in fact can be very misleading. Book-keeping records must be absolutely up-to-date and set out in such a manner that financial information for management accounting purposes is always available. What techniques do we have available to us for use in our practices?

Information for monthly partners or directors meetings

In order to know the current financial position of the practice it is necessary to have the following information:

Bank position
Overdrafts
Surplus

Fees positions
Fees invoiced this month
Fees received this month
Fees outstanding

Payments
Invoices paid
Salaries paid
Total payments for the month
Total income for the month
Balance

This information can be prepared by a book-keeper, accountant or administrative assistant. Forecasting and budgeting can follow with the presentation of a monthly budget statement.

(1) Monthly budget statements
These are presented in three columns showing the actual costs for the previous year, and forecast for the current year and the actual costs recorded at the day of the monthly meeting. Under budget figures are bracketed, over budget figures unbracketed and they are presented against known major cost elements which affect the control of the practice.

(2) Cash flows
Cash flows are particularly useful for assessing the past, considering the present and forecasting the future. It is advisable to estimate future expenditure for the office and also to do the same for expected income. The two can be put together to give an overall running balance and a forecast of liquidity and profitability on a quarterly, half yearly or annual basis. The cash flow can be

Annual budget control

Expenses	Forecast 1985	Actual 1985	Actual 1984
Establishment expenses	31 000	33 000	35 000
Travel	14 000	15 000	13 000
Salaries and consultants	303 000	330 000	298 000
Printing/stationery	11 000	12 000	9 999
Entertaining/advertising etc.	13 000	(12 000)	11 000
Telephone and postage	9 000	(8 000)	7 000
Insurance	22 000	24 000	16 000
Legal and accountancy	8 000	8 500	8 000
Cars	22 000	(21 000)	28 000
Repairs/renewals	900	1 200	600
Computers	10 000	14 000	6 000
Bank interest and charges	12 000	13 000	11 000
Bad debts	6 000	(5 000)	8 000
Pensions	19 000	19 000	16 000
Totals	480 900	515 700	467 599
Difference		34 800	
Income fees	550 000	594 000	521 000
Profit	69 100	78 300	54 400

This overall budget can be broken down into monthly or quarterly statements to show how the firm is performing against cash expenditure targets. Any overspending can be noted and acted upon if considered necessary. These figures are extracted from annual accounts and therefore to be of maximum use must be kept up to date.

Bracketed figures — below budget
Unbracketed figures — above budget

used both as a forecasting and a control document. It is highly suitable for architectural business where projects run over many years and can be flowed and predicted. In order to maintain precision in cash flows, it is necessary to prepare timetables of all projects which can be set out in a linear fashion. This enables the person responsible for their preparation to have a proper relationship of time and money on hand.

Practice running costs cash flow forecast

Expenses	Jan	Feb	Mar	Apl	May	Jun	July	Aug	Sep	Oct	Nov	Dec	Monthly average	TOTALS
Accountants	—	—	5000	—	—	—	—	—	—	—	—	—	416	5000
Bank charges	3000	—	2000	—	—	2500	—	—	5000	—	—	1000	1125	13500
Directors' salaries	8000	8000	8000	8000	8000	9500	9500	9500	9500	10000	10000	10000	8208	98500
Technical salaries	11000	11000	11000	12000	12000	14000	14000	14000	14000	13000	13000	14000	12750	154000
Admin. salaries	3000	3000	3000	3000	3000	3500	3500	3500	3500	3500	3500	3500	3291	39500
N.I. contrib.	2500	2500	2500	2800	2800	3000	3000	3000	3000	3000	3000	3000	2841	34100
Pension scheme	220	220	220	220	220	220	220	220	220	220	220	220	220	2640
Cars	1200	1200	1200	1200	1200	1200	1200	1600	1600	1600	1600	1600	1366	16400
Consultants' fees	1000	2000	8000	2000	1000	—	—	2000	3000	6000	5000	—	2500	30000
Phone	—	—	3000	—	—	3000	—	—	3500	—	—	3500	1083	13000
Rent	—	—	5000	—	—	5000	—	—	5000	—	—	5000	1666	20000
Rates	—	—	—	4000	4000	—	—	—	—	4000	—	—	666	8000
Total	42000	55000	60000	48000	52000	52000	40000	45000	55000	54000	44000	61000	46333	556000

This information is taken from previous year's annual accounts or cash flow. It is updated monthly. Actual costs can be printed in by leaving a space underneath. It can be compared with previous year, and bottom line monthly costs can be compared with income cash flow forecast prepared in a similar fashion below.

Income cash flow forecast

Job No.	Name	Jan	Feb	Mar	Apl	May	June	Jul	Aug	Sep	Oct	Nov	Dec	Total year	Fee remaining
2543	Hale Rd	3000	—	—	—	6000	—	—	500	—	—	500	—	10000	2000
2588	Moon La	—	20000	—	—	—	—	30000	—	1000	1000	1000	1000	59000	15000
2589	Wood Pk	—	—	36000	—	1000	—	—	2000	—	—	2000	—	41000	8000
2620	Hill St	30000	—	—	—	45000	—	—	—	4000	—	—	4000	83000	16000
2622	Valle Rd	—	—	—	10000	—	2000	—	2000	—	2000	—	2000	18000	10000
2625	New St	11000	—	2000	2000	2000	2000	2000	—	1000	—	—	—	22000	Complete
2710	Pool tr	—	11000	4000	4000	4000	—	—	—	—	—	—	2000	25000	Complete
2712	Park Rd	2000	2000	2000	2000	2000	2000	2000	2000	2000	2000	2000	2000	24000	48000
Total income		58000	40000	72000	51000	69000	41000	39000	31000	58000	68000	45000	81000	653000	266000
Balance		16000	(15000)	12000	3000	17000	(11000)	(1000)	(24000)	3000	14000	1000	20000	97000 (Profit forecast)	

(Income less expenses)
New balance
commenced (15000) 1000 (14000) (2000) 1000 18000 7000 6000 (18000) (15000) (1000) — 20000

From the linear timetable of jobs prepared previously and used for staff planning and allocation, a cash flow fee forecast can be prepared. Figures are entered in months when fee is expected, totalled for the month and compared with forecast of expenses for the same month, and the difference plus or minus recorded under balance. For the information of a financial director or bank manager a forecast of bank overdraft can be included as new balance. The cash flow is updated monthly and presented to the directors and partners meeting for comment. A gap can be left under each entry to include the actual amount paid and this can be used as a reference for future forecasting.

Minus figures are bracketed.

(3) Administrative management techniques for the control of money
Money can be lost and regained and it is more flexible to control than time. There are many well tried techniques which can help to improve your knowledge of how money is spent in your practice and what makes profits. Your book-keeping system is the source of all information on expenditure and income. The most common is the double entry system. From this source the annual audit is prepared and all quarterly and half yearly interim statements and balances can be communicated and budgets prepared.

(4) Job costing
This is a very important function of management accounting in all offices. It enables the architect to set up forecasts of probable financial and time performance on projects as soon as they come into the office. It enables the architect to set yardsticks at various stages of the building process, which can be used for comparison against actual performance. Performance is recorded through time sheets prepared regularly by the staff, which are then translated into money by multiplying by hourly or daily rates. The job can then be costed on a monthly basis and compared with the expected costs, and decisions can be taken on the facts presented.

To calculate the average man day or hourly rate which is needed to transfer forecast and actual time into money forecast as expenditure and actual expenditure, the following should be done:

Decide on number of days worked per year in your practice, say:	230 days
Translate that into hours, say:	1610 hours
Put in the number of staff working on projects. If partners do technical work some of the time make an allowance, say:	30 people
Put in the figure from last year's accounts which covers overheads for the year, say:	£400 000
Put in technical salaries for the year, say:	£420 000
Total costs	£820 000

Calculate average rate including
overheads per technical head per day:

$$\frac{820,000}{230 \times 30} = £118 \text{ per man day}$$

Average rate per hour $\dfrac{820,000}{1610 \times 30} = £17$ per hour

With these rates you can multiply them by time spent on projects to obtain job costs.

If you want to be more accurate and use man day costs for various levels in the practice, you can adjust the average upward or downward as necessary. If you are working on time charges then add in a percentage for profit.

Once you have the costs and you have put them against time you can then calculate job profitability and monitor progress against performance targets. You can fill in forms such as resources forecasts which can be found in the RIBA book *Resources Control*, or you can prepare histograms or graphs which visually communicate progress.

You should then know whether a project is on target or not. If it is wildly outside your forecast you should use the exception principle and take immediate action to establish facts and reasons why this has happened and then decide rapidly on appropriate action.

New methods and aids

All these management accounting functions used to be very time consuming and laborious. Nowadays we have microcomputers with spreadsheets which will manipulate tabular material. The procedure has become simpler and less arduous, and is really worth the investment. It enables senior people in a firm to see how the money is being spent, what is coming in, and what action needs to be taken to correct problems which could lead to serious situations well before they become a crisis.

Once the habit of management accounting is established, nobody returns to the bad old habits of looking in cheque books to see what has been spent, receiving irate letters from the bank

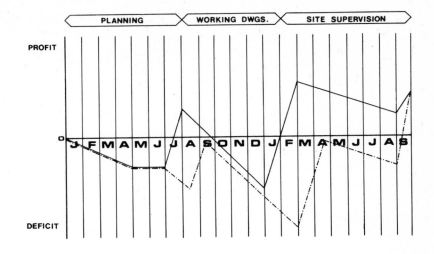

CASH FLOW

—— cash flow for normal RIBA stage payments
—·— cash flow if payments are delayed for two months

OPERATION
- to stress the importance of early payment of fee accounts.
- early payments or monthly fee agreements keep a job in the black and reduce overdraft levels.

about the overdraft, not knowing how much each project is costing or having no idea of income from year to year.

Collecting fees

Whenever architects get together they tell stories about how they have had problems in getting fees from their clients. Some of these stories amount to tragedies and others to success over great adversity. Why do we have difficulties in getting our fees? There are a number of reasons:

(1) The architect has not tied up the contract from the beginning and there are loopholes which the client can exploit to reduce the amount of the fee to be paid.
(2) Changes have been made either by the architect or the client which so alter the nature of the project that the fee for the revised work bears little relation to the original. Where the

revisions were not kept constantly under review the client can often absolve himself from payment of the revised fee.

(3) The client, finding something quite trivial which is wrong with the building, attempts to sue for negligence and avoids or postpones paying fees.

(4) The client actually has a valid claim for negligence but withholds a very high proportion of the fees unreasonably.

(5) The client does not pay the fees because he disagrees with the expenses.

(6) The client pays only part of the fee, not the full amount against the account rendered, keeping most of the fee in his bank.

(7) The client sells the project on to another party, informing you that you also have been passed on, but omitting to agree what fee should be paid. You are faced with an unwilling new client who wants to renegotiate the fee downwards.

(8) Bureaucracies will not pay fees if you do not carry out exactly the correct procedures.

(9) Bureaucrats will not pay fees because the contractor or sub-contractor has failed to perform well, and as their work is unsatisfactory, the architect also is made to wait for payment.

(10) The client is in serious financial difficulties and makes many complaints in order to delay the payment of the fee.

(11) The client does not pay the agreed fee in full, saying he will offer further work which is more valuable than the actual money outstanding. Of course this work generally does not materialise, or if it does, it becomes a series of abortive schemes which end up with the architect losing more money.

There are some very good rules which will help you to avoid difficulties with fees at the very beginning of a contract with a client. They are:

(1) If you can, make any new clients sign a memorandum of agreement. If a client will not sign this, you can presume that his intentions are not honourable.

(2) If he will not sign a memorandum of agreement but is honourable, he should exchange letters with you defining your appointment.

(3) If he will do neither, then forget the client however desperate

you may be for work. The odds are that you will be in a worse situation if you continue without either of these safeguards. You will either lose money or end up with large bills for litigation.

(4) Always clarify with the client the actual percentage of the fee and what expenses will be paid, and get this in writing. If you are going to agree a lump sum fee, make sure you relate the lump sum to a construction cost or some target which can be measured, in order that you can charge extra costs if the client deviates from your contract.

(5) If you are introduced to a client with whom you have had no previous experience and you have any feeling of suspicion, ask him what projects he has carried out in the past, find out who the architect/builder was and ask them about the client's performance, or if possible check the client's financial performance through your own bank.

(6) When the client wishes to deviate from the normal conditions and procedure, define precisely what services you will give and how much he will pay you for each separate service and relate this, if possible, to a timetable.

(7) When tying up an overseas contract, it is usually advisable to contact a lawyer who specialises in this type of contract, and also to ensure that you have adequate insurance cover through the various institutions who offer this service, so that if you do fail to get your fees there is some recompense.

(8) If you think the client baulks at large staged payments, negotiate smaller monthly payments on standing order or by monthly statements.

Book-keeping

Book-keeping is a necessary function in any office, however large or small. It is a continuing operation which, in medium and large size offices has to be attended to daily by permanent staff, whereas, in small practices, it is often done by either a part time book-keeper or the secretary to the practice who also has a book-keeping function. The principals of practices must ensure that this function is carried out by the right type of people who are prepared to be extremely meticulous and exact in everything they do, and who work methodically and logically through whatever system has been considered appropriate for the particular business.

The book-keeper's tasks are listed on page 115. The objective of these transactions is that proper records are kept of all financial events which affect the office, so that they can be used for management accounting, decision making and the annual audit.

Daily, monthly, quarterly and annual tasks are described in the section on day to day administration.

THE ARCHITECT AND HIS ACCOUNTANT

Not many accountants understand the business of architecture, and if you are going to choose one, it is best to go to an accountant who already has a few architects as clients. You may have to sacrifice the chance of your accountant recommending you as an architect to one of his clients, but I have seldom found that accountants are consulted when clients want to appoint architects.

Once you have selected your accountant, he must be educated in the way in which your practice operates because different firms have different philosophies and attitudes towards financing their practices. Once a relationship is established the most important service an accountant gives you is the annual audit. However, there are very many more services which can be offered as long as you ask for them.

I have found that accountants are very reluctant to sell you services which can be of use to you. You have to ask for them. The kind of services which an accountant can offer you are:

— Investment advice
— Partnership agreement advice
— Company agreement advice
— Personal taxation
— Personal trusts
— Property financing advice
— Student grants advice
— Student grants claims
— Attending negotiations for bank finance
— Management accounting systems.

Duties of a book-keeper

Daily	Banking
	Post
	Enter cash book and purchase day book
	Filing
Weekly	Enter time sheets
	Enter petty cash book
	Bank update
Monthly	Salaries — preparation and despatch
	Payment of office bills
	Staff expenses
	Fee accounts
	PAYE tax
	Bank reconciliation
	Close and control cash book, petty cash book, draft fee day book, fee day book, and purchase ledger
	Close time sheet ledger
	Prints journal
	Enter disbursements and balance disbursements
	Job monitoring
	Post general ledger
	Cash flow
	Working trial balance
Quarterly	VAT return
	Profit and loss schedule
	Trial balance
Annual	Set up files for new year
	Trial balance
	Prepare for audit
All the time	Set up new jobs
	Payment of petty cash
	Payment of cheques
	Fee account receipts
Balanced and entry books	Petty cash
	Cash book
	Day book
	Fees due book and draft fee day book
	Disbursements ledger
	Profit and loss ledger
	Access
	Staff expenses
	Salaries
	General ledger

Together with these services are the informal communications which you have with your accountant when you seek advice and enter into dialogue about financial problems facing your practice.

It is also very useful to bring your accountant along to meetings with your bank manager, particularly when you are embarking on a major loan or financial arrangement which will have tax and other financial implications. Very often what appears to be a simple and lucrative business arrangement with the bank can have extremely unfortunate tax consequences at a later date which can totally change the calculated profitability of the venture.

THE ARCHITECT AND HIS BANK MANAGER

It is wrong to think that you must court your bank manager. On the contrary, you should really ask yourself: 'Is my bank manager courting me?' The architect is the customer and the bank makes a profit out of lending money. The architect who keeps his account in the black is not a good customer for the bank. On the contrary, it is the architect who has projects and is expanding, who wants loans, and runs a fairly high overdraft, who is a good customer of the bank.

Most bank managers do not understand the business of architecture and need to be informed about it. The architect must therefore spend time showing the manager around his practice, explain how his projects are processed and the principles of cash flow as it affects his work. Bank managers should be kept informed by sending, say, quarterly cash flow statements to him, so that he can be warned of a period when the overdraft limit may be reached, or alternatively can put money on to deposit if there is a surplus for a short period. Spending time educating your bank manager in the special nature of your business will lead not only to a smooth and fruitful relationship, but may also result in recommendations from him to new clients.

TAXATION

If you want to run a business you must have an annual audit. This proves profitability on which taxes will be levied. Practically every architect in this country pays taxes whether from salaries, earnings, profits, buying of goods and services, property, interest etc. Taxes are levied by the state to raise revenue.to pay for services and the government delegates the responsibility for collecting taxes to the Inland Revenue, Customs and Excise, local authorities and the taxpayer.

Most business people do not understand the complexities of our taxation system and therefore employ a qualified accountant to advise on the legitimate methods of tax management for their firms and themselves. The main taxes affecting architects are:

Income tax Schedule D, cases I and II, which deals with incomes arising from trades, professions or other vocations (sole proprietors and partners). Other schedules and cases deal with such matters as interest, dividends and rents received. The tax due is normally paid in two equal instalments on 1 January and 1 July.

Schedule E (PAYE) deals with wages and salaries from employment (including directors' salaries). All businesses are responsible for the calculation of tax and National Insurance from employees and payment to the Collector of Taxes if the amount of an individual's weekly earnings exceeds the annual sum stated for the current year or if the employee has other employment as well. Each employee will have 'free pay' above which tax is payable. The Collector of Taxes will issue tax tables etc. on request. Payment is made monthly by the employer. Each individual partnership must complete an annual employer's tax return.

Corporation tax is payable by limited and unlimited liability companies on their profits. The rate of Corporation Tax has varied in the past and is considered in each Finance Act. The current rate is 40 per cent, although smaller businesses pay a reduced amount (30 per cent). Advance Corporation Tax (ACT) is payable at a rate equivalent to the standard rate of income tax when dividends are paid.

Value added tax (VAT) is a tax paid on goods and services sold. A few items are exempt (e.g. insurance, medical services) whilst others are zero-rated (e.g. fuel, food and all new buildings). Most items, however, are subject to the standard rate of VAT —

currently 15 per cent. VAT is paid (or refunded) quarterly and the amount is simply calculated by deducting the VAT charged on all purchases and allowable expenses (except personal items and cars) (input tax) from the VAT charged on chargeable sales (output tax). Businesses with a turnover which is likely to currently exceed £20,500 per year must register for VAT with the local Customs and Excise (VAT) Office. If your main sales are zero-rated, it pays to apply for voluntary registration.

Inheritance tax now replaces capital transfer tax. To help small businesses the value of small businesses is reduced by 50 per cent when inheritance tax becomes assessable and there is a threshold of £71,000 below which no inheritance tax is payable. Thus small businesses with a value up to £142,000 do not attract inheritance tax if these are your only assets. Any value above this will attract inheritance tax but the payment may be spread over eight years (thus lessening the chances of family businesses selling essential assets or having to close down).

Capital gains tax (CGT). If you sell or give away assets (e.g. premises, including business goodwill, shares, cash and other valuables) and your real or notional gain in any one year exceeds £6300, you are liable to pay CGT at 30 per cent on the difference between the price you paid for the asset (adjusted for inflation after April 1982) and its current net value. If you dispose of an asset prior to seven years before death, no tax is chargeable. Small businesses may also benefit in two ways:

(1) If an asset is sold but the proceeds are used to buy another asset within three years, payment of CGT may be deferred until you finally dispose of the qualifying (roll-over relief).
(2) If you have owned a business for ten years, you may elect, at the age of 60, to dispose of the assets to a maximum gain of £100 000 without payment of CGT.

The sale of your sole residence does not attract CGT but if the business occupies part of the property this may be subject to CGT.

Rates on business premises attract no relief (unless granted by the local authority for start-up schemes) and, like domestic property, are assessed annually on the net rateable value of the property. Water rates may also be based on the net rateable value of the property or charged on a meter reading.

Rates are payable in April and October of each year but payment by standing order or direct debit (on a monthly basis) is normally accepted, if requested, at the beginning of each year.

Taxation for partnerships and companies

Tax law for companies is mainly based on the Income and Corporation Taxes Act 1970, the Taxes Management Act 1970, the Capital Allowances Act 1968, Capital Gains Tax Act 1979 and annual Finance Acts.

Every individual who receives income of any kind is under statutory obligation to complete a return of income each year. In a partnership the form for annual return is the responsibility of the senior partner. In companies it is the directors' duty; personal responsibility for accuracy cannot be avoided.

Tax inspectors make assessments of individual liability for tax in accordance with the tax payer's return of income and supplementary details. A copy of the annual accounts of the business accompanies the return.

Individuals are entitled to appeal against Inspector of Taxes' assessments, the appeals can be settled by correspondence or a meeting with the Inspector.

If agreement cannot be reached, the appeal can be heard by General Commissioners or Special Commissioners. General Commissioners are leading local citizens who judge the case on merits and aim at a fair decision based on the facts. Special Commissioners are civil servants who concentrate on complex tax issues.

Appeals can be costly in professional advisers' time. A decision of the Commissioners is binding on the Inland Revenue and taxpayer. If there is a dispute on a point of tax law the matter can be referred to the courts and onwards through the Court of Appeal to the House of Lords.

Tax not paid on the due date is subject to interest, currently at 11 per cent.

PENSIONS

Why we need them

Those young people who are concerned about their pension would not usually seek entrepreneurial activities by starting up in architectural practice. The risk is high and a person who is over-concerned about pension at an early age does not have the right attitude to private practice.

This having been said, everyone in private practice should nevertheless make provision for old age, and must put money aside for this purpose. Those working as staff in large firms will either join the firm's pension fund or opt for the state system. Staff in small and medium sized firms would have to stay in the state sector because most small practices cannot generate enough money to make a pension scheme worth while.

Generally pensions are a specialist field of investment and expert advice should be sought from a good broker before any commitment is made. Your accountant may also advise on the advantages and disadvantages to you in tax relief and other benefits which change annually.

In order to provide quotations for a company or partnership pension scheme the competing companies will need certain information. They need to know everyone's name, sex, salary, date of birth, date of entry into service, and what scale of benefits are required. The latter can vary between different members of staff according to their needs.

The main decisions are related to a person's salary level and what proportion of final salary will be the basis of the pension. Usually this is anything between a half and two thirds of final salary. Principals of the firm are likely to have their own pension scheme based on the current most beneficial scheme available.

The ages of retirement can also vary between 55 and 65 according to personal requirements.

There are many special benefits that can be sought, such as bonus schemes, schemes that are unit trust linked etc.

EXPENSE ACCOUNTS

It is often said that directors or partners live off the firm's 'perks'. Expense account living became prolific in the 1970s as a means of overcoming high taxation which could then take 83 per cent of a partner's top slice income.

The Inland Revenue requires that, to be allowable, these expenses must be 'wholly exclusively and necessarily incurred in the performance of their duties'. Some benefits, including cars, are likely to incur a liability to personal income tax.

For many firms entertaining, cars, house parties, sports activities and second homes on expenses are an essential part of their business. However, it is essential for a firm to have a policy to cover these activities, as expenses can quickly eat up profits and can certainly be abused. What is the best policy? There are three courses open to you — round sum allowances, scale allowances or pay as you go.

The first two are practically impossible to control: to the wasteful it would mean so much to squander each month, to the cautious it could diminish enterprise. Some would end up with a profit and the honest person could end up out of pocket. I therefore opt for the third system and keep a regular check against a budget for reasonable control.

This system relies on the honesty of individuals. Unfortunately there are those who would never think of helping themselves to the petty cash but would happily abuse an entertainment allowance.

Finally there are times when it is beneficial to the firm for a principal to be accompanied by a spouse on business trips. This should always be a policy decision and not be left to individuals. The consequences of loose control can lead to jealousies and galloping expenditure, even to dissolution of partnerships.

PROFIT SHARING SCHEMES

Profit sharing schemes and co-ownership of the business have always been an attractive incentive. However many schemes can be complicated to administer and your accountant and solicitor should therefore be consulted before setting up a scheme.

Profit sharing for staff based on distribution of a certain percentage of annual profit is also popular. A percentage has to be fixed (say 20 per cent) and then the lump sum is divided up and distributed to staff. There are three methods of division:

(1) based on salary
(2) based on performance and judgment of directors
(3) based on setting up targets and measuring achievement.

Having attempted all three systems, I would say that there is no ideal system and you must be prepared to accept disappointment from some staff while others will be delighted.

7 Insurance

You may occasionally meet architects in small practices who say that they do not believe in insurance and prefer to carry their own risks. If they were sued for professional negligence, they would claim that they were men of straw and not worth suing. There are those who have told me that, as they run very personal practices with only a few people, they could not possibly be negligent or make the type of mistakes which would lead them to being sued by their clients. There are yet others who say they have sufficient funds to meet any claim that could possibly be made against them on any matter which could arise from their professional occupation. With the increase in litigation in our society such people are likely to become a rare species.

On the other hand, there are those who take completely the opposite view. They appear to have been petrified by their insurance broker into taking out every insurance cover possible for every type of risk at, of course, an enormous cost.

FINDING THE BEST INSURANCE FOR THE PRACTICE

Choosing the best insurance is a matter of common sense, of balance and of measuring reasonable risks. First of all, it is important to get good advice and you do need to choose a reliable insurance broking company. It may well be necessary to use different brokers for different types of insurance, such as the specialist area of professional indemnity insurance. Essentially you need a broker who is willing to go out to a range of insurance companies to obtain quotations, and who is not solely motivated by the commissions which are offered by insurance companies and which could influence his choice to your detriment.

Insurance can be split into five types:

(1) Personal
(2) Partnership or company personnel
(3) Other practice matters
(4) Professional liability
(5) Decennial insurance.

Personal

The architect in business will normally have a home and other assets which will need to be insured under normal home and contents insurance and, if he has a home mortgage, he will probably have an endowment life policy related to the mortgage. It is very important that these insurances are effected because they could come into consideration during difficult times, when guarantees given to the bank by partners or company directors could affect their homes or other assets. It is therefore essential that these assets should be properly secured and insured for the sake of the practice.

Other insurances that are personal but which could affect your business are related to motor cars, boats, animals, caravans, house contents, valuables, health and personal accident and disability. There are insurances which provide combined security for all personal risks.

Partnership or company personnel

Partners or directors will want to take out insurances which affect them personally in their senior capacity. These insurances are taken out to cover risks which relate to guarantees, shares and financial loans to the company or partnership. The cover is taken out for all the senior people in the firm.

These insurances provide self employed pensions for partners and a self administered pension scheme for company directors and employees; temporary life cover on death of senior employed people; permanent health and private medical insurance to protect the firm from long absences of senior people and to avoid key members of the firm having long delays in obtaining medical treatment.

Other practice matters

The whole of the practice will have a multitude of risks that need insurance cover. These risks can usually be made into an inclusive 'all risks' policy administered by your broker.

The risks include: fire risk to the building ('fire and special perils') contents, theft, loss of money, loss through dishonesty of employees, loss from destruction of accounting records, inspection and breakdown of lifts and machinery, breakdown of computers and loss of computer systems records, loss of fees and additional expenses resulting from fire and special perils, liabilities to employees and members of the public, travel, staff personal accident, motor cars, site equipment and legal expenses.

I have found that it is always beneficial to pay additional premiums for consequential losses as these can be much greater than the initial loss.

If you absolutely refuse to go to brokers then it is advisable to act as your own broker and obtain the discounts and commissions which are available. This can take up much time but can lead to the satisfaction of getting a good deal for yourself. Magazines like *Which?* are very helpful to those who wish to go it alone.

Motor cars

Car insurance is the area where most claims tend to arise. If the office has many cars, then a block insurance can be very competitive, although very costly if one of your staff or partners is a 'rogue' driver. If your insurances are very high because of problems with substantial claims, then it may be worth thinking of having the cars of 'rogue' drivers hired under contract.

In order to ensure that you get the best value from so many insurances, they should be reviewed once a year, when a responsible person in the practice should meet the broker or representative of the insurance companies to go through all the insurances at one time, so that on a certain day of the year you pay for all your insurances and confirm any arrangements for staged payments throughout the year. In this way you would probably spend only one day a year on the subject, and give yourself more time to get on with the real work of the architect.

PROFESSIONAL INDEMNITY INSURANCE

Professional indemnity (or PI) insurance is so specialised that there are only a few brokers who are expert in it. It is therefore best to get quotations from all of them and use these to negotiate the best deal for yourself. Every year when renewals are made you should check the market again to see that you are getting a fair deal.

All policies have 'excess' clauses which means that the insured bears a specified proportion of every claim. If you decide to opt for a higher excess you may well be able to reduce the premium paid.

PI policies also provide that the insured architect hands over the right to conduct all litigation to his insurers, who will process the case while you get on with running your business. Some claims arise from clients who are in financial difficulties, or who are even straight rogues, and who wish to avoid paying fees by counter-claiming for negligence and breach of professional duties. If your insurer settles rather than fighting what may be a valid case this will probably go against your principles. But remember, litigation is costly in time and emotional energy.

Above all you should realise that, since most policies cover only claims made within the year of insurance, you will need to maintain a policy not only for the rest of your professional life, but also after you have retired, since although you can only be sued in contract six years from the date when the breach took place, in tort you can be sued in negligence up to six years from the time when the damage to a building occurs. A new Limitation Act may restrict this to a total of 15 years, but at the time of writing this has not been enacted.

Most architects' policies are written on a 'claims made within the year of cover' basis and not on a 'work done within the year' basis. Such policies afford no cover whatsoever for claims made outside the year of insurance.

There are a few basic rules that should be followed:

(1) Read the proposal form carefully. Get legal advice if you have any doubts about the legal interpretation of clauses.

(2) Fill in the proposal form carefully and truthfully.

(3) You must be certain of notifying your insurers of any *potential* claim, even one as trivial as a leaking roof. Otherwise the insurer can avoid the policy on the grounds of non-disclosure. Your duty is to disclose everything which would affect the mind of a prudent underwriter in granting or renewing a policy or in determining the premium.

(4) In choosing the amount of cover, work roughly on two to three times annual fee turnover. This should cover small practices, though large practices will have to do more accurate assessments to get the right cover.

(5) Look carefully to ensure you know what is covered in your insurance. You will not normally be covered for reimbursement of costs in defence of a claim, unless you have additional legal expenses cover, although of course if you are successful in your defence you will get an order for costs from the court.

(5) Have a QC clause in case you need independent advice on how the defence to your claim should be conducted, as this may differ from your insurer's view.

(6) If dealing with consultants, such as civil engineers or quantity surveyors, do not enter into direct contract with them but make sure that the employer engages them. You will then have no legal liability for them. You should advise the client to check that his other consultants are adequately insured.

(7) Make sure that your insurance covers retired partners and any past project carried out by the practice even before the current partners or directors were in charge.

You should realise that insurance companies, like any other business, need to make a profit each year. They will therefore seek to limit their losses and will apply well tried methods to mitigate claims.

Decennial insurance

There is another form of insurance now on offer which is called decennial insurance.

Many clients complain that if there is a structural defect in one of their buildings shortly after the final account has been settled, they find it is practically impossible to get the contractor to return to the site to repair the defects if there is any dispute about the responsibility for the defect. Disputes related to structural defects can last many years before an arbitrator or a court will decide on who is to blame. In the meantime the client can suffer the consequences of the defect for many years or will have to pay out of his own pocket for the repair of the building and then have to wait until legal settlement is made to recover the costs.

During this period the client may easily fall out with the architect, even though the architect is not responsible for the fault. The contractor will probably refuse to return to the site or may indeed be in liquidation, and the client may well therefore turn on the architect in an attempt to pursue his claim.

There is now an insurance scheme which helps prevent this unpleasant situation. This is called decennial insurance and was introduced into the United Kingdom in 1981. It provides a ten year named party cover against structural failure of all new buildings. It performs a similar function as fire insurance, enabling immediate reinstatement of damaged buildings so incurring the minimum delay and interruption to the client's business. The insurance company offer a ten year non-cancellable period of insurance and also a design and construction check from the foundation stage onwards that may forestall major problems at a later date. It is recommended that the insurance starts from the inception of the project so that checks on the design and construction can be made at the production drawing stage.

Not only does the policy cover damage to the building caused by defects in design, materials or construction; it also includes cover for subsidence, heave or slip of land. In addition it also gives the client protection for loss of rent and debris and contents removal.

The cost of this insurance is approximately 2 per cent of the total construction cost and is a once only payment (i.e. not annual). Special arrangements on many contracts can reduce this sum, and it can be taken out by the client or the tenant occupying the building. The client, as policyholder, can name a subsequent owner or occupier, which may be a financial institution or tenant, as the insured. It is advisable that the architect should mention this type of insurance to his client at the earliest time before design work commences.

Decennial insurance does not affect the architect's professional indemnity, except where subrogation rights were waived against the architect. Some of the additional premium required for such a waiver may be partially offset if the architect can negotiate a lower premium on his professional indemnity.

If you think there are special or unusual risks associated with one of your projects you can obtain a quotation for a 'top up' of your insurance.

Finally if you employ agency or ghosting assistants tell your insurers so that they are aware of this fact when the annual premium is agreed.

Indemnity insurance will always be an area of constant change. The present legal situation is a minefield for architects and other professionals in the building industry and the only safe way is through insurance.

8 The client and project management

CLIENT GROUPS

An architect in private practice will probably see himself as a commercial individual, operating quite differently from one in central or local government. An architect's style of business is likely to be dictated by the type of client who engages him, and the sort of work in which he specialises.

However, particularly in the last decade, because of market forces, many practices have had to change the type of work they do and have had to seek work from clients with whom they have had no experience in the past. The appraisal of these new markets and the decisions which must be made are discussed in the chapter on the marketing of architectural services. The aim of this chapter is to point out the advantages and pitfalls of working with particular client groups:

— central government
— local authorities
— statutory authorities
— housing associations
— private companies
— development companies
— institutions
— private clients.

Let us now look at these in turn to identify some of the advantages and disadvantages of working for these organisations.

CENTRAL GOVERNMENT

Central government employs architects in various departments of government who are career civil servants. Sometimes they carry projects through from commencement to completion, but often they delegate part of the project to outside private architects, and with government policy this is an increasing trend. The largest government employer of outside architects is the Property Services Agency (PSA), part of the Department of the Environment. The PSA, like other ministries, has a panel of architects on whom they can call when needed.

To get on the panel of approved architects, you apply, fill in forms, deposit brochures, and the system will usually ensure that most of the superintending architects who make decisions on which private architect to choose will enter your name on his list of approved architects. However, once this has been done there is no guarantee you will ever get work. Generally speaking, unless the superintending architect knows of you either personally or through some colleague's recommendation you are unlikely to be approached to carry out a government project.

However, if you are considered for a project, you will be called to the respective ministry or office to receive the brief, agree the scale of charges etc in the traditional manner or be asked to provide a fee submission in competition with other architects.

Nature of the architect's appointment

Often the architect is not asked to carry out design work as this has already been done by the Ministry architects, and the commission is instead to carry out detail design and production information and provide a certain degree of on-site supervision, for which there is a reduced fee which has already been laid down by the administration.

If you are engaged for the whole design project, there will probably again be a slight reduction on the normal recommended fee because there will be a certain design and briefing input from the ministry's own architects.

First encounters with the system

At the first interview, discussion will also turn on time and money, and this is the area where you encounter the first difficulties in dealing with government bodies. Money is allocated on an annual basis and there will therefore be certain periods of intense activity and other times when very little will happen because they are either running into a new budget or out of an old one. This can cause delays and stop–start working. Time targets are normally set for projects but they are hardly ever achieved because the financial constraints create time deficiencies.

Consequently in a reasonably managed office, when a team is allocated to a government job, it is unlikely that this team will see the scheme through from beginning to end because of cost cuts and time delays.

This means that you are forever re-engaging or re-organising project managers and architects as and when the scheme starts and stops over, perhaps, a number of years. Although these delays will often cause the cost of the project to rise, it is not always possible to recoup the increase since fees will remain fixed except for inflation. If there are delays and alterations it is very difficult to obtain more money for time spent in changes caused by political interference.

Movement of government officials

The other problem of continuity comes from the government side. Generally civil servants are regularly promoted or transferred and they often stay for only two years in one job. This means that the whole team, including the client has to be reorganised after perhaps six or seven months' delay on a project. Everyone has to start from square one again and of course this costs time and money.

The commitment

If you commit yourself to this type of work, you must sum up the consequences of the nature of the client's organisation, and patiently and firmly deal with the oscillations of workload which result from the government system of carrying out projects.

A recent trend highlights some of the problems: government offices have been asking contractors to carry out design and build tenders and projects. Generally speaking, contractors have to engage private architects to join them in a team, presenting themselves to a PSA selection committee who will expect that an overall lump sum design and build price will be agreed. This sum will be recorded and will be forever regarded as the target price. It would be foolish to believe, even if you won a tender of this nature, that the price or the time would be the same as that discussed at the original interview.

Such problems arise because civil servants are subject to political control, and fiscal expediency is usually most often exercised in the capital building sector to the detriment of the overall efficiency of the civil servants, professionals and contractors operating the system.

LOCAL AUTHORITIES

Until fairly recently local authorities were very extensive employers of private architects. Whatever the party in power, there was always a policy that their architects' department should never be large enough to carry out all the work necessary, and the surplus would go out to the private sector. Many architects have earned the whole of their income from local authority work. Even during the period of cut backs, private architects are still being used on the most unpopular form of work which is rehabilitation and maintenance.

Local government structure

Local authorities comprise various specialist departments, such as the architects' department and housing department, who report to a chief executive, who in turn is responsible to the elected representatives. They are also subject to the normal government annual budgetary system and consequently have the same problems in administering budgets on an annual basis as does central government.

Private architects employed by local authorities are often those who are working in the locality, have been able to get their names on the panel and, by personal contact, have persuaded the authority to employ their services when needed. The usual method of employing a private architect is to give him instructions for the whole project from briefing through to completion, and the RIBA recommended scale is often used as the basis of payment and the RIBA's Architect's Appointment for the conditions of engagement.

Inter-organisational difficulties

The first problem encountered by private architects is that those who carry out the briefing are not likely to be the users of the building. Unfortunately departments do not get together to co-ordinate the information which they wish to pass on to the professionals, so the project may be very far along the plan of work before briefing changes are made by the departments who are going to be managing the building when it is completed. The private architect may often have to redesign all or part of the building at his own cost in order to meet the changed requirements.

Another risk in local government is that during the scheme design there may be elections and the opposition may win and cause delays or make changes to the scheme. Another cause of delay is changes in government grants or in policy when new bulletins and circulars are sent to local authorities which may have a fundamental impact on the building design. Again, these changes cannot be absorbed by any increased fees and the architect has to bear the cost.

At the tender stage delays may also occur when, if the project is subject to a government grant, it has to go to a ministry for a final decision on the expenditure. This kind of delay can be anything from three to six months and it has an impact on the management of the project from the private architect's point of view.

The lack of continuity upsets the effective management of the project, there is discontinuity of staff involvement, and time and cost targets are changed, which in turn cause further administrative delays when they need to be adjusted.

The architect working with a local authority has to be prepared to be very flexible in managing these projects and should preferably be able to handle several projects at one time so that some continuity of staff involvement can be maintained, and cash flow and liquidity can be balanced.

Methods of dealing with central and local government

If you want to survive the central and local government system there are three courses of action worth pursuing:

(1) Always prepare a meeting agenda and take your own minutes and circulate them after the meeting, even if the civil servant administrator also takes notes of the meeting. Record all changes of brief or design, and confirm acceptance with reference to the extra work to be done and the consequential effect on your remuneration.
(2) Always bring a timetable for the project to meetings and when the inevitable changes are made immediately draw on and display the effect of the delay; have this accepted and distribute an updated timetable after the meeting.
(3) Always have a cash flow chart for the project, including building costs and fees due. When changes are made immediately calculate and demonstrate the effect on the cash flow, preferably in red ink. Confirm revised cash flow and change in cost immediately after the meeting.

If these actions are taken on a regular basis the officials will always know of the effect of changes, delays or a moratorium in terms of time and money. When you submit your fees to perhaps a finance officer who is new to the team, he can consult the file and find the evidence for which he needs the authority to pass your fee.

STATUTORY AUTHORITIES

Large corporations such as British Gas, The National Coal Board, and health authorities, run on annual budget systems for long term projects similar to those found in Central and Local Government. They normally employ a group of architects in their own architects' department, and carry out most of the maintenance and small extension works associated with their day-to-day requirements. Large projects are often placed with private architects, who are

subject to the same difficulties as working with any large
government body — delays, budget changes, staff movement etc.
The private firm must be capable of managing these changes and
still make a profit despite the difficulties. There is less political
interference in the case of statutory authorities and therefore the
chances of a straightforward throughput are that much greater.
Working for these organisations is therefore likely to be more
profitable than in the case of other government bodies.

HOUSING ASSOCIATIONS

Since the Housing Act 1964 when the housing association
movement was given great impetus from the government, architects found regular work with housing associations, societies and
other bodies mainly funded by government finance but some
by charitable funds. Some large housing associations have their
own in-house architects who work on specific projects and who
liaise between the development officers of the housing association
and the private professional firms employed on the projects.

Housing associations obtain grants from the Housing Corporation which is the main funding vehicle provided by the
government. These grants consist of allowances which vary
according to the needs of the housing association and the projects
allocated. Architects are put on a panel and asked to carry out
projects as and when sites are found and applications are made to
the Housing Corporation for the scheme to be funded.

Abortive work

This system leads to a considerable amount of abortive work for
architects, with often fruitless searches for sites. Even if a site is
identified and prepared for development, by the time the
application has passed through the various processes of the
Housing Corporation the site could very well have been purchased
by a private developer and all the work carried out to meet the
Housing Corporation's initial criteria is wasted. This can be very
costly for the private architects who have no means of recovering
the cost of the abortive work.

Administrative delays

If a project can survive the initial process, it is often approved but no money is allocated until a certain time has elapsed and the Housing Corporation releases the funds. Thereafter there are even longer delays while valuations are obtained from district valuers and solicitors are engaged to purchase the site. Consequently the early stages of a housing association scheme are full of uncertainties and can be very time consuming for the architect.

Approvals process

If the scheme is approved by the housing association and is processed through the planning system, the design can still be changed by the Housing Corporation's officials in order to meet the cost criteria which are not easily definable. Likewise, after tenders have been received the same kind of reduction estimating, cutting of costs and delays can occur before the project gets on site. It is very difficult for an architect working in this system to claim for delays and changes even though these are often outside his control. Consequently it is practically impossible to forecast any profit on this type of project. There has been a tendency recently for the Housing Corporation to choose only small schemes of up to 15 units and these are subject to the same administrative procedures and delays. Schemes of this size can really only be carried out profitably by very small practices.

Experienced housing associations also demand architects with in-depth knowledge and experience of their form of specialised housing. It is therefore difficult for a new practice to meet this need. Only the most experienced and well managed practice has a chance of negotiating their way through the system with a profitable success.

PRIVATE COMPANIES

Private companies are often wholly owned by the directors, or by members of a family. Architects employed by these companies are usually private practitioners with some family or personal relationship which has led to their appointment. The architect is often asked to carry out work not only for the company itself, but also for personal projects of the directors, and so he often gets quite close to the group of people or family who are running the business.

What the private company client wants

Generally speaking, the briefing is simple and the needs of the company are straightforward too. They want the simplest building, in the shortest time at the lowest cost. The money they are using is either personal funds or direct guaranteed loans from the bank, and there is therefore pressure on the architect to work at his most efficient. With these types of constraints, particularly on time, it is often true to say this is the time when the architect can make his maximum profit. What is more, as long as he is not involved in changes of mind and family or local feuding within the company, these projects can lead to the most satisfying work for the architect.

The risk

The greatest risk with private companies is that they can become insolvent, overreach themselves, or get taken over and sell you and your project to a bidder who may be a stranger and with whom you must establish new relationships.

DEVELOPMENT COMPANIES

Objectives

There are both private and public development companies. They all work basically on the same principles: to find sites, get the greatest potential from the site in relation to its location and land use, to let the buildings, to sell on to an institution or to hold it as an asset and as the basis of future loans for further projects.

Architects' employment

Development companies often employ a group of private architects and encourage competition among them. They are often influenced by estate agents' surveyors who will also recommend their architect friends for projects. The business is generally extremely volatile. As time and money are the main constraints projects have to be completed very rapidly, despite difficulties with planning permissions and letting. This type of commission can be the most profitable.

The management of a project is often divided among the client's surveyors, the architect, a management fee builder, and other people engaged by the client to join the building team. It often requires the architect to take firm control in order to ensure that good design is achieved in the fastest time and at the most reasonable cost.

INSTITUTIONS

The corporate developers

Before 1973 very few insurance companies or pension funds were involved in actual development. They normally purchased investments or funded developments on the advice of their surveyors who were either in-house or private professional surveyors. After the 1973 property collapse many of the institutions were left with uncompleted projects and sites, and they therefore entered the development business and operated very similarly to development companies.

The client's representative

The real difference in being employed by institutions is that normally you are dealing with salaried staff who have no financial involvement in the projects, rather than personally involved developers. Under this regime projects take longer to process and are under more rigid controls. It is in the long term interests of insurance companies and pension funds that buildings should be constructed to a high standard and therefore architecture of a good design quality is possible. Institutions are normally good payers and usually work to the RIBA recommended scale. They also treat their professionals with respect and understanding.

Institutions are normally funded by the subscriber members, and because of the rapid expansion of these organisations, architects are engaged either to extend their existing buildings or sometimes to design new institute headquarters.

Management techniques for dealing with these bodies

The first impression that the architect will have is that the learned persons who form the building committee have very little idea of the normal type of service provided by an architect or the roles of the professions and trades which make up the building team. Time spent on explaining these and the procedures by which building projects are managed is never wasted.

This task may have to be repeated several times throughout the project because annual elections of the institute will change the complement of the building committee. It is therefore essential to liaise with an employed officer, probably the secretary of the institute, to ensure continuity.

Architects are frequently made aware of the institute's lack of funds and are asked to assist in raising money and providing presentations to benevolent bodies or at fund raising functions.

Difficulties are often encountered in settling a final brief but thereafter, as long as money and time are controlled, the institute members act as a sympathetic and supportive client. If, however, there are delays or costs are exceeded, much time is spent in obtaining committee approval for changing the brief.

Generally this type of work requires careful attention to detail and consequently more money is spent on production information.

There are compensations however. It may well be that an institute will be opened by a member of the Royal Family, as patron, and the building team will get considerable publicity from the event.

PRIVATE CLIENTS

The smallish type of work which private clients require is usually a loft conversion or a house extension, and probably this kind of work represents the majority of the projects which are given to small practices.

There are other clients who are entrepreneurs or owners of

residential and commercial property, who do one or two developments per year, either for income or to let, and then sell on to an institution. These clients also trade in property by buying and selling, sometimes with the advantage of a planning permission which has been obtained for them by the architect.

There are of course some wealthy individuals who want a large private house or a substantial conversion. One example of this type is the overseas client requiring property in the UK.

Finally, there is the client who runs his own business or factory with private capital, and wishes to expand, so requiring architectural services.

The common factor among all individual clients is that they are usually using their own money and therefore financial targets must be adhered to because there is no further money available.

Appointment of the architect

Some individual clients phone the RIBA and use the Clients' Advisory Service; others rely on directories or other impersonal sources. By far the majority of individual clients appoint architects by recommendation, through family, friends or business associates. In most cases the individual client is probably asking the architect to do the one and only building project in his or her lifetime. He can therefore be classified as the 'naive' client.

Other individual clients have built up experience with architects. When this type of client approaches you, it is well to find out why they have not continued with their previous architect.

The procedures for securing your appointment in a proper and businesslike manner must be carefully controlled and communicated to the client so that he fully understands the commitment and the conditions of engagement under which you are going to work.

Time spent in carefully explaining the whole of the building process and the type of services which you and others may have to perform to achieve the client's objective is time well spent. It is particularly important that everything is confirmed in writing to the client. Often, the client will not have the ability to type letters and is reluctant to write any message to you. It is essential to insist that there is some record of your offer and his acceptance and instructions before you start work. Otherwise you will not be paid full fees for your work and you will receive nothing if the scheme aborts.

Additionally, it may be necessary for the architect to make enquiries as to the client's financial resources for the enterprise before commencing work. This can be checked through various investigation companies or through your bank.

In the case of the individual client you cannot be too careful in making sure that he will keep promises and meet payments promptly.

Design procedures with individual clients

Many individual clients do not understand drawings or plan sections and elevations. They may not even understand a perspective. It is vital in the early stages of design to communicate your proposals clearly to the client, so that both he and his family have an unambiguous idea of what is proposed. This situation is fraught with communication difficulties and good records of meetings and decisions are essential to prevent future problems.

The planning process also causes difficulties, particularly in domestic situations where there are relationships with neighbours who may object to the proposals and the whole scheme becomes charged with emotional conflict. The architect must tread very warily in this situation and have an understanding of the planning procedures, particularly consultation procedures which can cause considerable delays to applications. If the client does not understand the procedures and problems, he will tend to blame the architect for delays.

Production information and tenders

After planning permission is received much time should be spent with the client in making sure that every detail has been agreed. Although the client often wishes to postpone such details until he can actually see the building, the temptation to yield to this wish must be resisted. Indecision can lead to extras creeping into the project causing extensions of time and increases in cost which the client generally cannot afford.

The actual tender process is usually based on specifications and drawings and generally no quantity surveyor is involved. In this case the architect will be expected to have a detailed knowledge of costs and be able to advise on the selection of contractor, and on the tenders, and he must be able to analyse the costs. The choice of contractor is usually a painful activity as it is difficult to find good small builders who are well organised and can manage the building operations. Often the client will recommend builders known to him. Generally after investigation they prove to be unsuitable. However if the architect is weak and allows these people to quote, a disaster is in store.

Supervision

The insurance firms specialising in professional indemnity report that most of their claims relate to the supervision of small works contracts.

Usually the individual client has either run out of money or refuses to pay as the building is not what he expected and has not reached the desired quality. The builder may have gone bankrupt and the only person who is answerable is the architect. In many cases it is impossible to avoid this situation arising, particularly if insufficient care has been taken in the earlier stages of the procedure. However, if the earlier stages are meticulously managed, the chances are that the project will be completed at the right price and on time.

Although it is seldom that an individual client requiring a house extension will ever require the services of an architect again, you may have made a friend who will recommend you to others.

In the case of the individual businessman the same procedures are essential. Very often the client's business will grow and be successful and this is the type of client who may well help to build up your practice.

9 The practice and project management

For some years it has been traditional in the UK for architects to view themselves as controllers of the whole of the building process from inception to completion. The architect is appointed by the client and initially the client will be dealing with the senior architect, director or partner, according to the size of the firm, except in the case of a one man practice or a small practice of up to five persons.

In large practices the architect who receives the initial instructions is unlikely to see the job right through as the job architect. Normally, the principal will return to his office and consult with his partners or co-directors as to who should be the job architect, partner or associate on the project. Once that decision has been made, it is assumed that the job architect concerned will see the project through from feasibility to completion. But this need not be the case. The job architect may leave the practice or become involved in other work, particularly if there are long delays in the purchase of the site or in obtaining planning permission. There may therefore be two or three job architects during its period of development.

CHOICE OF SYSTEM OF OFFICE PROJECT ORGANISATION

Today, however, the problem is not as simple as that stated above. Depending on the size of the office, there are different conflicts to be overcome before a satisfactory system can be evolved for the management of a project passing through any size of office. The choice open to architects is one of three systems. They are:

(1) Traditional whole man team
(2) The process method
(3) Functional specialisation method.

The *traditional whole man team* is the system used by the majority of small and medium sized practices in the UK.

When a project is commissioned the architect will take the brief, carry out research, and proceed to design the building on his own or with some assistance. The architect will meet the client and obtain acceptance of the scheme design and will carry out all negotiations and make submissions for planning approval. The architect and his assistants will then be engaged in the detail design and the co-ordination of consultants and sub-contractors' detail designs before building up a team of assistants to prepare production information under his direction.

The architect will convey all decisions in drawings, specifications or schedules to the quantity surveyor who will prepare a bill of quantities for tendering by contractors.

The team of assistants will eventually complete all the production drawings. The architect will manage the tender process and organise the appointment of the contractor and commencement of the operations on site. The architect and his assistants will then carry out periodic inspections, attend meetings, produce extra information, appoint sub-contractors and co-ordinate consultants' information as the job proceeds. The architect will supervise the commissioning and 'snagging' of the building until practical completion and hand-over is achieved.

During the six month maintenance period the architect will deal with defects, advise on settlement of the final account, carry out end of defects inspection and issue the final certificate.

The *process method* relies on a project manager (who may be an architect) who takes the client's brief and communicates the information to members of the building team.

The project manager briefs the design department architect whose team designs and presents the building to the client, obtains planning permission and then hands over the information to the project manager.

The project manager proceeds to instruct the technical design and production department to prepare production information. The information may then pass to the quantity surveyors who would be responsible for co-ordination of consultants' information into a bill of quantities.

When the bills of quantity and production information are complete, all the documents are passed to the contract supervision department by the project manager. This department will monitor the project through the tender, project planning, operations on site and completion stages, with the project manager overseeing the process and retaining contact with the client who eventually takes over the building.

The third method, the *functional specialisation method*, is similar to the process method from the management and procedural standpoint.

The design department is broken down into groups of people with detailed specialisation, i.e. people who will only do planning or elevations or interior space planning. They have great in-depth knowledge and ability in their chosen speciality. The work will be co-ordinated by a design architect into a whole design. The project manager will liaise with the design architect to ensure overall objectivity.

The production department is staffed by specialists in parts of the building, e.g. windows, plumbing, cladding or finishes of varying types. They are only involved in making their specialist contribution to the whole building and are co-ordinated by the head of department and the project manager.

The contract supervision department have staff expert in different construction techniques and finishes, all of whom apply their specialist knowledge to that part of the building under construction at any one time, again co-ordinated by the project manager. In large projects run on this style of management there is an on-site architect's office.

The whole operation is carried out by high quality experts in all the building specialities.

Let us look at the advantages and disadvantages of the traditional system in (a) the small office and (b) the large office.

TRADITIONAL SYSTEM IN THE SMALL OFFICE

In the small office it is normally the case that the sole principal has given initial advice or worked on a project from the earliest moment when his client considered building or buying a site. He has probably put a considerable amount of work into the scheme before he actually gets the commission. The scheme will be of a size normally carried out by a small office and the resources available would be capable of meeting the requirements of the client in terms of time, cost and general objectives.

Provided the small practice intends to remain the same size, the principal will be deeply involved in the design, development and all the negotiations related to the management of the scheme through the various statutory bodies. It is unlikely that the principal will do all the production drawings, but he will certainly be involved in sketching out and ensuring that all the details drawn up by the technicians or junior architects in his employment are strictly in accordance with his requirements for that job.

The control and the communications will be direct and personal with the client, statutory officers, staff in the architect's office, the consultants who may be employed and the contractor on site. The client will rely entirely on the ability, health and financial resources of the principal.

As long as these three elements are at their optimum, the project has an excellent chance of success, with the minimum of management input from people other than those who are directly concerned with the project. However, failure of any of these three elements can lead to a disaster for the client.

Ability to perform will depend on the time and resources which the principal can put in to that particular scheme. The architect should be experienced in the type of project and not be learning at the expense of the client. As long as the architect has all round ability and experience then the prognosis is good.

Health is always a problem to small practices. If the senior assistant is ill, then perhaps a quarter to a third of the work force could suddenly be out of action, with serious consequences for the client. There are no reserves and very little flexibility if the principal is indisposed. Temporary staff are too costly for this size of office. Most principals and senior assistants in small practices work very long hours under a considerable amount of stress as they are normally working to the limits of their resources.

TRADITIONAL SYSTEM IN MEDIUM AND LARGE OFFICES

The medium or large office, which employs the traditional team or whole person method, encounters different problems when applying this system to project management.

A commission will normally be received by a senior or junior partner, who will refer the project either to an associate or senior member of his own team within the office or to another partner who has the responsibility for allocating staff to projects. If the scheme is simply absorbed or taken in with the intention of the partner's own team carrying out the project, this could lead to problems of resource allocation throughout the period of the project.

If the scheme is allocated by the partner responsible, the introducing partner may not necessarily get the people he prefers. The allocating partner would decide on the job architect and the team according to who is available at the time, or employ more staff. The management of the project in the large office would require a greater degree of office organisation in order to establish the essential requirements of the team method where the job architect should have face to face relationships with clients, local authority officers, contractors etc. with whom he will have dealings throughout the project. Depending on the size of the project therefore, a partner, associate or senior job architect or even a junior job architect would have to maintain these close contacts with all those involved, to ensure that the project is properly managed and he will need the back up of a team of architects and technicians who will have sufficient ability, enthusiasm and consistency to ensure that information is produced on time and to the standard and quality required by office policy, and to the financial targets set at its inception.

However, because of the discontinuity of larger projects, particularly those being backed by government or bureaucratic organisations, there are frequent problems as to the availability, reliability and consistency of staff on a project. The project proceeds erratically with different staff changing the design, detail etc. in a chaotic path to the completion of what can only be an unsatisfactory building.

The process method for medium and large offices

The second method of managing projects through the office is called the process method. This derives from the principle that every project has three distinct processes: design, production information and site supervision. These processes require three distinctive, specialised qualities in the people who are going to undertake the work.

Designers are often weak on technology and site supervision. Technologists are not always creative designers. Site supervision these days requires very strong types of personality, with good legal and technical knowledge to deal with the problems of running contracts.

The importance of overall strong management

In order to maintain continuity through these three processes, there would be a project manager or architect who would follow the scheme through from beginning to end to ensure that the client's intentions are achieved in the completed building.

Disadvantages

The split into three departments may appear alien to architects who have been trained on the assumption that they will be actively involved in all stages of a development. In this type of office, they would find that they would be involved in one of three departments, and would have to prove their expertise in that department before they were moved to another.

Design of the building by the design department must be faithfully followed by the technical department. Likewise the site supervisors must be able to appreciate the building as a whole from the technical information, and see that this is accurately applied during the erection of the building.

If the project manager fails to see that this happens, clients' requirements can be distorted and lost completely, and eventually the building will be of poor quality and not meet the original brief.

If a project manager leaves the firm, then there can be serious consequences during the time before he is replaced, and while the new project manager is settling in.

Additionally, the directors in charge of the design department, technical department and supervision will make varying claims for staff and resources according to workload and pressures, which might well upset the balance of work flowing through the practice.

Advantages

The advantages are that each department develops its own expertise and allows a greater depth of professionalism and knowledge to be developed in each department member. This particularly relates to building types in a design department and technical specialities in a technical department. The system allows the individuals in the practice to have greater in-depth knowledge of their particular contribution to the whole building. It also allows planning of projects to be more structured and controllable because, in the first two stages of the process, there are only two departments' workload to consider, not a multitude of teams as in a traditional system. It allows more detailed planning of drawing production and internal office cost control. This system should produce a continuous and more consistently high standard of product.

Functional specialisation method for large practices

This system is only suitable for very large practices. It is founded on the principle that every person in the practice must have in-depth expertise in clearly defined parts of the process or technical areas affecting the building. There will be specialists for feasibility studies only, and specialists on plans but not elevations. There will be negotiators who will be specialists in planning negotiations and handling statutory bodies.

The technical areas will be staffed by specialists in specifications, windows, plumbing, structures, heating, electrical engineering, cost evaluation, interior finishes etc.

Site supervision in turn will be split up into on-site inspectors and contract managers, all with considerable expertise in their particular field. Each project will be introduced to the firm by a project director who would have a job architect or project manager who would monitor the scheme from beginning to end to ensure continuity, communication, and maintenance of the brief and the standards originally decided with the client.

The system is only really effective when applied to a very high standard on large buildings.

Disadvantages

The disadvantages of this system are quite apparent. There are very expert people looking at one particular area of the building and exercising great skill and detailed knowledge. When many of these people get together to put the whole building into a complete design, there must inevitably be conflicts of interest which have to be resolved by a very strong project manager who must be equally expert and well trained in his particular art. Communication of design and production information is a major problem. The mass of information produced on such projects is usually greater than with the other methods, and needs a strong administrator to exercise control and orderly progress. Co-ordination of information is also difficult because the project manager or job architect must be not only a generalist, but also someone who can weigh the claims of the specialists involved in the whole process.

Advantages

The product, if properly co-ordinated and managed, is of excellent quality. Virtually everything will have been thought of in detail by experts and communicated in first class drawings, specifications and documentation. Normally, the contractor will get everything from the outset of the contract. The real secret of this process is strong management by highly trained managers.

To summarise, the whole person team system is suitable for small and medium sized offices, but becomes unmanageable as the offices and projects get larger. The process system is good for medium sized offices and some large offices and allows greater flexibility and ease of management. The functional system is only for the very large firms, usually multi-disciplinary, offering services on large complex projects.

HOW THE BUSINESS DEALS WITH DESIGN

Design is the core of our service and of all our activities in taking a project from conception to completion. It is the activity which remains unchallenged as an architect's job.

From the business point of view it is the most difficult to control in time and cost because it is our most creative activity, the one which we like the most, the area of greatest personal sensitivity, into which we put our greatest emotional energy.

Many books have been written about the management of design to help architects to put the multitude of factors concerning design into an order which is manageable. These procedures have been helpful to many, particularly the designers who have previously used an instinctive approach to design, whilst it has helped the more methodical to see the process as a co-ordinated activity. These methods are also very helpful for design team working and for those very large projects where the planning of exterior design, interior design and landscaping are specialities of different members of the design department.

Who designs buildings in your office?

'The architects, of course,' you may say, but which architect? The one who has the most time available for this task, the principal, the associates, a design department, the job architect?

This decision will differ in all practices. In this area everyone has a different approach.

In the small practice design may be done by the principal only and must be carved out of the available time. The lone practitioner will probably find himself designing buildings outside normal working hours in a period of peaceful contemplation, away from the phone and those requiring day-to-day decisions from him. A well organised person could allocate a fixed time for this work per day but it is a hard decision not to be available to clients and builders throughout the working day.

In the medium sized office not all the principals will have time to design. Those who love the design activity may have to make a big sacrifice for the sake of delegation and the development of expertise within the office. Design may be delegated to one of the principals who will supervise the design associates or job architects, and ensure that the office design policy is applied to the client's needs in this sector of our work.

Clients are likely to be sensitive about the personal design attention they receive from the office of their choice and therefore the designer, at whatever level, should be involved in development meetings and have a face to face relationship with the client to get the 'feel' of what is needed.

Sometimes good designers react against business people, they feel threatened and misunderstood, they do not think they are given enough time to do their job properly and are sometimes regarded as impractical people who only put pretty pictures on paper. These attitudes have to be managed by the principal and the qualities of practicability and beauty have to be combined to satisfy the client's needs.

In the large practice the design activity may be incorporated in the structure in various ways. There could be a design department, or each project team could be assembled with a designer, and as the design develops more technical people could be included to build up total team management by the designer or project manager. Design is unlikely to be done by most of the partners or directors because they have predominantly administrative, management or marketing tasks. Some large practices have outstanding principals with a flair for design and in such a case those principals will keep to design activity but will need other principals to give management and technical support.

How does the business deal with design time?

How long does it take you to design a building? That is the impossible question which faces principals running an architectural business. Of course it all depends on the type and size of building, who will design it and how much money there is to spend on it.

Scheduling time for design is a tough task. Some design tasks are solved quickly and simply whilst others take a frustratingly long time to evolve. Design also requires the approval of many people, the client, his staff, the local authority, possibly conservation committees, the Royal Fine Art Commission and many others. These bodies only approve the general design. Detail design which usually follows can take an inordinate amount of time to process, often through many departments in a large client organisation.

In managing time to be spent on design you have to balance the time demanded by the client, which is often too short, and that required to satisfy the designers, which is frequently uneconomic in relation to the fee to be paid. Finding the right balance is a vital task for the principal in charge of the job. There are many clients who love being involved in the design process and can take up too much time on design, others can wear out the designer in chasing a multitude of ideas or changing their minds after planning permission and starting the whole process again.

Therefore design cannot be left to natural processes. It has to be managed, time-tabled, planned out as an office activity, with targets set and controlled, and final decisions obtained.

How do we control design costs?

Our fee scales usually allow payment for the design process to be broken into three stages: outline, scheme design and detail design. The total fee is divided into 15 per cent for outline design, 20 per cent for scheme design and 20 per cent for detail design, making a total of 55 per cent for design processes alone. This only leaves 25 per cent for periodic on-site inspections and 20 per cent for production information, one of the most labour intensive and costly processes in the office.

The 55 per cent for design does include the cost of management, negotiation and technical input. It therefore follows that the profit element must come predominantly from the money allocated to design, and hence this is where most cost control must be exercised to ensure a profit. The small percentage left for production information is hard to make profitable. Some practices defer some production information provision to the on-site stage but, in my opinion, this is uneconomic in the long term as it wastes staff time, and leads to inconsistent involvement in the project.

Production information is most economical when it is done in one co-ordinated operation, with all the consultants', specialists' and sub-contractors' information brought together at the same time and completed to a programme. Design input at this stage should be minimal if the previous stages have been thoroughly performed. Different jobs have radically varied design periods. We can only apply common sense, personal understanding, and the disciplines of time and cost control to help us to achieve satisfying designs at a profit.

What sells our designs?

If you have a good design and you present it badly you will not receive approval and you have therefore lost time and money.

At the beginning of every project and just at the time when a suitable design solution evolves, it is worth thinking about the most appropriate form of communication for presentation to various bodies for their approval.

Should you use printed paper showing your design in plan/ elevation/section in the formal way without colour, knowing that the approving body will fully understand what is being presented to them, or do you need the addition of colour, shadows etc?

Is a perspective needed? Should it be a photo-montage, a realistic drawing, an impressionistic water colour; should it be viewed from the ground, bird's eye etc? Does the client need perspective to understand the scheme?

Is the scheme so vast, complicated or reliant on its juxtaposition with other buildings to warrant a model?

The good managing architect will ask all these questions and arrive at the most appropriate answer. From the point of view of time and money, the model costs most and takes the longest time to produce. Perspectives are cheaper but you may need more than one. Formal drawings rely on experienced interpreters.

Design is a vast subject on its own. I have tried to illustrate some of the business problems associated with our main activity to get the right design for our clients at the minimum time and cost to ourselves, because this is the area of our greatest expertise for which we should receive our best reward.

10 Architecture is a volatile business

CRISES

No business stands still or does not have crises. Crises usually come from external events which are outside the partners' control. All you can do is to react and take action to mitigate loss or perhaps achieve a gain from the situation facing you.

Crises which occur internally are of a different nature. They can be the result of a long period of tension or disharmony which comes to a head as the 'last straw'. Senior staff movements can cause major disruptions which affect the quality of your services.

The most frequent changes that require flexible management are those introduced by government through annual budgets, and by commercial clients who experience liquidations, mergers, take-overs and abandonment of projects at crucial stages.

In many ways these crises are minimal compared with the effects of national and international booms and slumps. How do these affect practice?

BOOMS AND SLUMPS

There are always booms and slumps, periods of transition when the business climate is changing from boom towards a decline in business activity. Then there is the opposite transition when out of a period of recession business starts to liven up and we have the transition from slump to boom.

The real question is how can these swings of the pendulum be managed so that the business preserves its equilibrium and can accommodate the sometimes radical changes which can occur in a very short period. To some people the essence of the business is survival. To others it is taking advantage of change. Nowadays we often hear people complaining about these radical changes, pleading for the government to level out the swings of fortune. But this is unrealistic. The swing of the pendulum is part of life and we as managers have to be able to adapt to it, take advantage of it, weather the storm and maintain a balance.

Let us now look at the characteristics of booms, slumps and transitions from slump to boom and boom to slump.

Slump

There have been two recognisable slumps during this century: the late 1920s and early 30s, and the middle 1970s into the early 1980s. In the building industry there have been many mini booms and slumps over the past twenty years. Cuts in government expenditure, particularly those affecting capital projects, have been responsible for slumps in the building industry, and consequent loss of work for architects. In the private sector the business climate affects capital expenditure in startling ways. Normally there is not a gradual rundown. The effect starts with changes in the stock market and interest rates, lower customer expenditure leading to shut downs of factories and large pockets of unemployment. The first reaction is to cut down on capital expenditure which is the life blood of our business.

Boom

The most notable boom in the last twenty years was from 1970-3 when the government thought it could increase prosperity by increasing money supply and encouraging private enterprise. This created a very artificial property market and many architects during this period were extremely busy, as the public and private sectors were spending capital at a tremendous rate, which of course inevitably led to a very sudden collapse in 1973.

Booms are normally noticed after they have actually occurred. Everyone experiences an increase in activity. Offices start to get more work and want to expand. The euphoria is infectious and business activity increases in all sectors to a point when the inevitable fallback has to occur. Problems related to rapid expansion will be discussed later. This is a period of security,

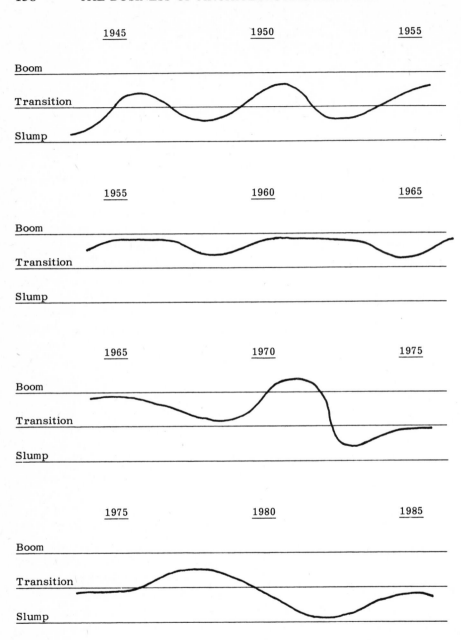

excitement, confidence and achievement but by the nature of our society booms do not last for very long.

Transition from boom to slump

This transition can be the most painful and it requires the greatest skill to manage. Sometimes the boom changes to slump virtually overnight, as in 1973. At other times there is a gradual move from boom to recession as occurred in 1979 and 1964.

Obviously the first signs of transition mean that the workload decreases and staff have to be dismissed. It is always a painful and difficult process. Problems related to premises, sudden downturns in cash flow, superfluous equipment and restructuring of the whole business are all parts of this process. If the recession is gradual you can have time to reorganise and re-adjust the whole business. If it is sudden, then the task is much more difficult and traumatic.

Those who have practised in the UK since 1970 will be well versed in this procedure. In this period there has been a sudden slump and a gradual recession into slump. The management of these changes is of a quite different nature to the opposite transition from slump to boom. Often at the end of a boom there is an overrun when there are a considerable number of projects on site and cash is still flowing in, but there is a noticeable diminution of projects coming into the office.

The cash is still being spent to meet the extra work created during the boom and yet the signs are ominous and cutbacks have to be planned. The most expensive element in any office is staff and this is the first task to be tackled. During a very busy period, some of your staff who were promoted at the earlier part of the boom prove not to be as good as you hoped, while other new entrants have outstanding qualities. The decision whether to make old staff redundant and retain new bright staff is painful and very difficult as often directors and partners may differ from one another in their view of the effectiveness of the staff under them.

There are obviously empires to be protected, diminishing jobs to be retained, and the difficulties of consequential reorganisation after staff have left. As well as this, there is the overall morale of the office which can be adversely affected during the period when the principals of the practice are trying to decide the new size and structure of the practice and size of premises they must shrink into.

Cutting a lot of the extra facilities which could be afforded in a boom often has a noticeable effect on staff morale, particularly as premises shrink and everyone begins to work more closely together in new teams. The direction of the office has to be maintained and reinforced during a period of collective depression and change in staff. Therefore, when this type of change has to take place and the office shrinks, people go, salaries level out, rises are less, work is more competitive, fees are lower, competition within the office itself is intense. This requires probably the greatest management skills to weather the storm and come out intact, so that you can make profits in the midst of recession and be prepared for the upward transition which will inevitably come.

Transition from slump to boom

Often a period of transition is the easiest period to manage. If you are coming out of recession and business is picking up, there is more workload, money is easier to borrow, you are operating from an optimistic economic base and people are not exhausted from overwork. New staff have to be employed, people within the firm may have to be promoted to take on new responsibilities. Extra premises may have to be obtained, more furniture purchased, greater capital expenditure against the promise and expectation of greater workload and profit.

The first question when work increases is whether you have sufficient funds to finance the operation. Very often after a recession there is a conservative and cautious atmosphere regarding the lending of money for new projects which may be in advance of the general boom which will affect the public perhaps in a year's time. You may go to see your bank manager for more finance in a period when most of his customers in general business are still in the depths of, or just recovering from the recession. This means that you have to be very persuasive and confident that your forecasts are going to prove correct so that you can raise enough money to fund the new expansion. Perhaps the hardest task is to persuade your sources of finance that expenditure now is going to reap rewards in the future.

Usually after the recession there are plenty of staff available and when you advertise you are inundated with applications. Regrettably this is not always the ideal situation. You begin to realise that the best people are still employed, even during a recession and those who are applying for jobs are inexperienced or are people other firms have decided to discard.

As expansion occurs you will need new premises. This often causes much difficulty and debate during a period when you want to concentrate your efforts on the new work coming in. If you are in a building where you have already let out your surplus space to others, then it is sometimes possible to get some back, if the appropriate provisions have been made in the lease. However, it often means that, because of the expansion, you have got to set up small branch offices in buildings nearby and this also requires a total re-think of your organisation and structure.

The choice between setting up small branch offices and moving the whole organisation into a single large office is very painful and comes at a time when you are intensively engaged in the new expanding projects. The leasing, purchase and equipping of premises is very capital intensive and, at these times, capital is often needed to fund the projects which are pouring into the office. As a result, even though work is pouring in, you will experience cash flow difficulties and will have to obtain medium term loans or arrange for monthly fee payments from clients, probably at slightly reduced fees overall in order to maintain liquidity during this period of expansion. You must also remember during this period that transitions leading to boom eventually result in booms leading to transitions, perhaps in turn leading to recession, and you may in a few years be back to the workload from which you started.

STAFF — EFFECT OF BOOMS AND SLUMPS

Most architectural practices have different levels of staff:

— associates and senior architects who are responsible for large jobs or teams in the office
— job architects who look after projects from commencement to completion
— architectural assistants who are either recently qualified architects or architects in training
— technicians, some highly qualified with in-depth technical knowledge and others who do technical draughting.

On the administrative side there is often an office manager or senior secretary responsible for administration, secretaries, typists, receptionists, telephonists, accountants, book-keepers, general office assistants and information officers.

There is perhaps another way of looking at grades in the office: those who are managers and those who are responsible for carrying out individual skilled tasks. Managers can be anyone from job architect upwards including office manager, senior secretaries, accountants and information officers.

Staff account for approximately 50 to 70 per cent of the total expenses of an architect's office. It is this area where, in a period of recession, the biggest savings can be made. How do we set about such a task? First a list of staff should be prepared, showing for each individual their qualifications, duties, current projects and the time span of those projects, their salaries and length of service, and details of their personal background.

Then the workload has to be studied, with a reasonable forecast of future projects, and a structure drawn up relating to the realities of what the office will be doing over the next year. This in turn must be related to the expected cash flow over that period. This should identify any shortfall in cash which would have to be met by reduction in staff or premises.

When the new structure has been drawn up and staff costs checked to meet the cash targets, then the most difficult task is to assess each individual, their potential, and whether or not they should stay in the firm. Each staff member should be assessed in terms of ability, performance, potential for development, the possession of special skills and personal behaviour, e.g. appearance and punctuality. The personal background of the staff should also be looked at. Married people are more likely to stay with you when the recession turns to boom. In some cases redundancy may lead to hardship. When this assessment has been carried out, then comes the difficult moment when the choice has to be made by the principals as to who stays and who will fit into the new structure.

The overall principle must be that the people chosen to remain in the structure must in the end make up a balanced and effective team. There must be some compassion exercised in these choices, particularly in choosing between the married person with children and a single person. This is the most difficult of all management decisions.

Administrative staff present a more difficult problem because it is often less easy to measure performance. Some administrative staff occupy key positions and you cannot afford to lose them even though their workload may reduce because of the recession.

One of the first tasks is to look at the ratio of administrative staff to technical staff. In the best offices the ratio should be 1:4. In some offices 1:5 or 1:6 can be achieved. In other offices, because of the nature of the practice, the optimum ratio may well be 1:3. If the ratio in your office is between 1:3 and 1:5 and you feel the staff are fully employed, then you probably have the right balance. If it is less or more then there may be some serious problem ahead.

It is always difficult to judge the effectiveness of secretarial work because of the nature of our business. In very small practices secretaries will do book-keeping, reception and information duties. In larger offices, where greater specialisation takes place, it is much more difficult to combine jobs in order to reduce staff.

During periods of boom, secretaries often get salary increases in line with the rest of the office until their salaries are well above the market level, but are doing a job which could be done by someone at a much lower salary level. This is one of the areas where difficult judgements have to be made. Is the higher paid but experienced secretary more valuable than someone less experienced or loyal? If the expensive secretaries must be retained then it is important that they take on more duties to fill up their time and to provide the essential services to the office. In periods of expansion this is no problem as you can fill in from below with younger secretaries and typists. In a period of recession it may be the best policy to have expensive secretaries doing more jobs effectively and efficiently than to have younger, less experienced people who may be cheaper to employ. However, if cash is the most important problem, the sacrifice may have to be made and the expensive secretaries must go.

Obviously flexibility and adaptability must be linked with proper attitudes to business survival. Often there are difficulties in reducing a book-keeper's or an information officer's time from full to part time as the work decreases, and *vice versa* as it increases. Some people are quite pleased to take on a part time job; others will leave and you will have to replace experienced staff. It is always difficult to find people of quality to fill these specialist jobs.

The other problem that may affect reduction in staff is when the firm is multi-disciplinary and has engineers and quantity surveyors within the organisation. It is well known that engineers and quantity surveyors need more projects to keep the same site team busy than architects. Therefore when a reduction in work comes, the quantity surveying and engineering sections may well have to take bigger cuts than the architects'. The problem then is whether there are enough people left to provide the same service which was probably originally set up during a boom period. How this is handled will depend on the position of the principal in the overall hierarchy of the office, as it is obvious that the quantity surveyor or engineer directors would argue very strongly for retention of staff. The main criterion should be establishing a realistic structure for the current circumstances.

In periods of expansion it is often necessary to expand the number of engineering and quantity surveying staff at a greater rate than the architects. This could lead to an imbalance in the type of services offered. The balance of disciplines in an office must be carefully monitored to see that the overall objective of the office in providing a multi-disciplinary service is maintained so that the office does not acquire a reputation of being predominantly one discipline.

PREMISES

The next item to be considered must be premises. As you reduce staff so your space requirements are less, but unfortunately this is likely to coincide with a period when there is a surplus of office space generally on the market. You are unlikely therefore to recover fully your investment by letting out surplus space. It is also not very lucrative when you have to pay tax on this income at the highest rate and the residue is so small as to have no effect on your cash position.

It is sometimes better to give up premises entirely, than to sublet in the hope that you will need the space again in the future. It is often found that because of the provisions of the lease, you cannot regain possession of the premises when you need them. New premises can be obtained when the trend turns towards a boom, as often the architect is working approximately one year ahead of most other businesses and can therefore negotiate a favourable lease and an attractive rent while the slump is on.

The disadvantage is that you may have to move the whole of the firm into new premises with all the changes and costs which result from this decision. If premises are owned and have to be let, it is better to get a lower rent and let the premises out on licence on the terms that on six months' notice you can regain the premises.

In a recession it is obviously not good practice to sell a freehold in order to realise cash. Generally it is better to use your freehold as collateral against borrowing during the tough period, and take advantage of the increase in value which normally occurs when premises are revalued during boom periods.

Equipment and office installations present a different kind of problem. The equipment may well be leased and it is difficult to break leasing agreements. If you do own equipment it has normally little or no resale value. The first principle, therefore, of the flexible office is to have equipment, furniture etc. which is easily moveable, can be stored away when not needed and re-used rapidly when circumstances change.

With fixed installations like computers it is sometimes better to install more work stations and abandon drawing boards in order to take up less space and improve productivity, rather than continue with methods which may be less costly in the short term but less efficient in the long run. Again, the choices may be difficult as in periods of boom there is much duplication of equipment but in slumps you cannot afford to pay for equipment standing idle and occupying valuable floor space. In these circumstances it is better to get rid of the equipment, since when the turn around comes new types of equipment and better methods may have been developed.

CLIENTS

Clients' behaviour during slumps must also be taken into consideration. Many clients, particularly private developers, sense when architects and other building professions are short of work. They are usually anxious about their own businesses and they pass on this anxiety to others by demanding more competitive fees and performance time, lower tenders and general economies all round. These economies impinge on all members of the building team and lead to more economic and intensive working practices.

From the foregoing it is obvious that whatever situation you are in, whether boom, slump or transition, the management of a firm has to change to face new challenges and keep an overall balance in the business so that it continues as an effective professional service.

11 Other businesses for architects

THE ARCHITECT AS A PROPERTY DEVELOPER

Many of the great architects in history, such as Robert Adam, were property developers. They speculated in buying land, building and selling for profit. Many were successful and we have heard about them, but many more have been unsuccessful and have ended in bankruptcy. One of the most outstanding developer architects of today experienced bankruptcy before he found the way to make a fortune. The architect who wants to be a developer must be someone who likes taking high risks for high rewards. Architecture alone takes most of a busy practitioner's time. To do development work as well means that somewhere you must make a sacrifice, unless you want to work 24 hours a day seven days a week.

The first essential in property development is to have a source of finance. You can obtain this either by making direct approaches to banks or financial institutions, or by working with an estate surveyor who can find sites and arrange funding of projects. Of course, he also expects to get the letting or sale of the completed development. Many developers started as estate surveyors, as they are probably closest to the point of action.

If you are a member of the RIBA and want to practise architecture and do property development it is advisable to inform the RIBA under the new Code of Conduct of what you propose to do. Once your operation has been registered you are free to act in any legal way you like.

The second essential of successful property development is to find a site in the right location because location is everything in property development. If funds are limited, you may not be able to buy prime sites. Therefore you have to take a bigger risk by working in secondary locations. If you find a site and want to carry out a development, the following example shows the basis for appraising the viability of the development.

Office development appraisal

*Date:*1 August 1985
Address: Newtown

		£
Site purchase		
Site (net)		1437485
Stamp duty	(1.00%)	14375
Legal fees	(0.50%)	7187
Agent's fees	(1.00%)	14375
Other costs		5000
Gross site costs		1478422
Development costs		
Quantity surveyor's estimate (gross sq.ft. 31000)		2150000
Professional fees	(13.00%)	279500
Contingency	(2.50%)	60988
Demolition		10000
Total construction costs		2500488
Finance cost		
Site finance	13 months at 9.00%	149647
Building finance	12 months at 9.00%	113788
Void finance	6 months at 9.00%	194192
Total finance costs		457627
Letting costs		
Letting fee at 15.00% estimated rental value (ERV)		46875
Promotion costs		25000
Total letting costs		71875
Funding expenses		
Developer's legal costs	(0.50%)	27174
Developer's agents		
Costs	(1.00%)	54348
Fund's legal costs	(0.50%)	27174
Fund's agent's costs	(1.00%)	54348
Fund's stamp duty	(1.00%)	54348
Total funding costs		217392
Total costs		4725804

Returns

ERV 25000 sq.ft. at £12.50 per sq.ft		312500
Investment yield =	5.75%	
Total investment value		5434783
Residual profit		708980
% of cost =	15.00%	
Yield on cost =	6.61%	
Net area as % of gross =	80.65%	
Break-even rent =	£10.87	
Rental cover =	2 years 3 months	
Site value.		1437485

All interest compounded quarterly, on building half rate
VAT excluded on all fees
VAT excluded on building costs

This table gives residual land values over a range of Estimated Rental Valuations (ERV) and yields to give a percentage profit on cost of 15.0% & cost/sq.ft of £12.50

Yield %	ERV =	12.00	12.25	12.50	12.75	13.00
5.50		1453018	1532173	1611328	1690292	1769257
5.75		1286316	1361847	1437569	1513291	1588821
6.00		1133538	1205826	1278305	1350784	1423264
6.25		992966	1062393	1131821	1201439	1271057
6.50		863266	930023	996780	1063538	1130295

If you can show that your development will be profitable and the site (ideally prelet) is in a good position, you can normally get sufficient funds on varying financial arrangements for development. They are as follows:

(1) You may go for a straightforward loan from the bank for a fixed term or a special loan for a project where interest is paid on an interest and capital repayment system.
(2) You may go to a fund where you can borrow the money and arrange for the interest to be rolled up to the end of the project if you propose to sell the development to the fund when it is let. Then the interest is deducted from the final figure.
(3) You may get a prelet for the site, sell it on to the fund and have it valued on the basis of the first rent, complete the development and take the profit.
(4) You may purchase a site, borrow all the money from the fund who expect you to pay the rent of the building if it is not let, and then you get out once it is let and the valuation can either be made when the project begins, or on the basis of the rent you get when the building is let.

On some specific industrial projects, some merchant banks may be prepared to have special forms of equity finance where you share in the ultimate profits, but they keep some of the equity.

While carrying out these kind of transactions, it is good to have a chartered surveyor working with you.

If you are successful, one of the biggest problems is what to do with the very large profits you may receive from one development which are totally out of scale from year to year with what would be a normal income. There are various government schemes where money can be invested quickly in order to reduce the tax payment at the end of a successful year.

Another form of property development for architects is to buy one's own office building, occupy part of the building and sublet the rest. This is particularly useful if the firm has a pension fund which can be used for the purchase and then gives an assured rental which can help with partners' and other people's pensions in later years.

You may even find that, in looking for a site for your own house, you can buy a house with a large garden, or simply a site, where you can develop more than one house. This has the great advantage that whatever income you get from the development can be put against the cost of your own house. The following example shows how attractive this can be.

Capital gains tax is receivable on the profit from the sale of the two houses; your accountant will advise. You would take out a mortgage to pay off the balance outstanding on your own house.

THE ARCHITECT AS ESTATE AGENT

The combination of estate agency and architecture makes sense in many ways. Solicitors are opening property shops in which estate agency and conveyancing services are performed, and architecture as an additional service could be very attractive to purchasers of property. Also the agency attracts customers with land who can be advised on development potential and possibilities of getting planning permission in one visit.

However, estate agency is hard work. Great patience is needed to deal with difficult customers and there is much abortive work before a sale is made. On the other hand, it can be more profitable

Residential development appraisal

Site for three four bedroom houses: one for architect owner occupier, two for sale freehold.

Site cost	£90000	
Stamp duty	900	
Legal fees	450	
Agent's fees	900	
Interest for one year @ 15%	13500	
Total		£105750
Building cost		
3 houses of 150m^2 @ £400 m^2	£180000	
Professional fees @ 10%	18000	
6 mths interest @ 15%	13860	
Total building cost		£211860
Void finance cost three months @ 15%		11160
Funding cost/bank charges		1000
Sale of two freehold houses @ £150000 each		
Agent's fee	10500	
Promotion costs	1000	
Total selling cost		11500
Total development cost		£341270
Sale of two houses		£300000
Cost of own house		£ 41270

than architecture and there is a more constant cash flow if you are successful. Architecture shops are opening up in high streets offering combined services but it is too early to tell whether it will become a popular service.

THE ARCHITECT AS BUILDING COMPANY DIRECTOR

There have been many great architects who have both designed and built, Robert Adam being one of the outstanding examples. Now that architects can also act as company directors it is not a great step to undertake contracting work as well. Because most building is carried out on a sub-contracting basis the personal qualities needed are management and organisational ability.

However, to go into a competitive tendering system it is necessary to employ experienced estimators. Depending on the scale of operations, an architect with business and management skills can fill the role of building company director with success.

It is possible that the incentive of high rewards for building work could reduce an architect's enthusiasm for the less profitable pre-contract work.

THE ARCHITECT AS EXPERT WITNESS AND ARBITRATOR

Those architects who have an interest in the law and its procedures may be tempted to move into the field of building disputes. A number of architects have studied law and become barristers. They earn their living dealing with building contract disputes as expert witnesses, advocates or arbitrators.

The work is spasmodic: sometimes there may be nothing to do for weeks and at other times there will be a considerable pressure, with the need to study briefs, appear in court or at arbitrations or conduct hearings, leading to busy weekends. The people involved in this work are few and tend to know each other and form something of a professional fraternity.

The Chartered Institute of Arbitrators runs courses for practising architects who want to spend some of their time conducting arbitrations (ideally architect/arbitrators should still be involved in day to day practice).

SUMMARY

These days an architect has considerable choice of ways to earn a living in the construction industry. The nature of architectural training and the type of service architects regularly provide means that they are very useful people in other professional pursuits and associated building activities. The basic requirements of the business of architecture — the ability to imagine the objective clearly, define it to others, plan and organise work, co-ordinate and communicate, and control time and money — are applicable to any human enterprise.

12   DOs and DON'Ts

- DON'T accept anything but excellence from your accountant, solicitor or bank manager. You will also perform better for your clients when you exercise the same policy on yourself.
- DON'T use a solicitor or any other professional who has not had experience in dealing with architects' specific problems, unless they are prepared to pay you for giving them the opportunity to learn.
- DON'T have a solicitor or an accountant who is a close relative. Most weekends are ruined this way and you can't sack them.
- DON'T let your overdraft go over the limit so that your bank manager contacts you. If you think it is going over the limit, tell him, and tell him how you are going to get it down again.
- If you make a capital gain on a property deal DON'T spend it all. Put money away for capital gains tax. If you collect rent, remember unearned income tax is at the highest rate, so put money in reserve and avoid nightmare tax bills with interest threats and charges.
- DON'T pay rent for your offices if you can afford a mortgage and end up owning your own office. If you do buy your own office and wish to borrow money from the bank don't let the bank talk you into a medium or long term loan. Try to set up a property account on an overdraft facility and pay back that way. It saves money, tax, and is a more flexible vehicle as you can increase or decrease the repayments as and when you feel it necessary.
- DON'T leave the valuation of shares to be settled by the

shareholders when a director wants to leave the practice. Appoint the company accountant to independently value the shares and make his decision final.

- DON'T give up manual accounting for computer systems until they have run in parallel for at least two years, otherwise you end up in an awful mess.
- DON'T keep changing your accounting or budgeting system. All control information is only of use if it can be compared with some previous or forecast figure.
- DON'T employ cheap book-keepers. They always create more chaos than the money you save in the lower salary. DON'T let your accountant's assistant do it either. It will cost you dearly.
- DON'T leave the book-keeping until later; do it regularly — weekly if possible. At the end of the year when the auditors arrive their costs per hour are often more than yours.
- DON'T employ book-keepers who won't adapt to new systems. They can spoil the management accounting procedures by delaying the processing of information.
- DO try and employ book-keepers who can prepare management accounting information. It makes the job more interesting and shows them how to make the figures work for the firm.

CLIENTS AND CONTRACTORS

- DON'T advertise in newspapers. All you get are hundreds of small enquiries which take up your time and produce no worthwhile work.
- DO carefully select your advertising media and choose those that get on to your potential client's desk. If you then want to convey a message you have less than ten seconds to do it. Someone at partner or director level should be in charge of marketing and sales, should approve all media outlets and the content of any promotional information. Marketing is not a job for the staff.
- DO employ marketing or advertising agents but make sure you give them very clear instructions and make them aware of the limits of your market, otherwise they will give you marvellous but quite impractical ideas, and produce presentation material at great cost but of no use to you.

- DO have lunch dates with clients but DON'T postpone meetings because you cannot fit in lunch. When you want to see a client, see him as early as possible.
- DO be friendly to contractors, sub-contractors and suppliers but make it quite clear where you define the limits on offers of gifts.
- DO go as guest of contractors to social occasions if you know lots of other architects will also be there. Sometimes return the hospitality; it keeps relationships in balance.

STAFF MANAGEMENT

- DON'T draw up permanent organisation charts. Just use them temporarily to explain relationships at meetings and discard. Rigid structures lead to rigid people with rigid attitudes.
- DON'T give the partner or the senior staff in the administration the authority to interfere with the production line of the architect's office. The drawings and specifications have priority, the administration serves and supports the line.
- DON'T have just one assistant with another assistant below him. It is better management to have two to four assistants reporting directly to you, with less passing-on of communications to others.
- DON'T have more than four people reporting to you if you have external relationships with clients etc. Those people reporting to you will not be able to obtain adequate guidance and decisions to maintain their efficiency.
- DO give job architects the whole job. DON'T interfere with their major decisions unless you are sure it is in the client's interest to do so.
- DO try and employ a responsible architect as a deputy in a small practice, whatever the cost, so that during sickness or periods of holiday you can rest content, as can your clients.
- DO delegate everything you think someone else in your firm could do for you. This helps your staff to grow and gives you time to make the firm grow.
- DO have partners who share all executive responsibilities and jobs equally and with whom you enjoy working and have complementary skills. If you cannot establish that kind of relationship then have a traditional pyramid structure where one person finally makes and

implements decisions. If you have equality in mind then take turns at being the final decision maker.

- DON'T have a system where each partner or associate has one secretary. Most architects who are actively in practice cannot keep one secretary fully occupied. A good experienced secretary can be responsible for the running of the administration as well as being a secretary thereby saving the office the cost of an office manager.

- DO fire people when necessary. Keeping someone unsuitable is unfair to others. It's unpleasant but absolutely necessary when the whole office's optimum performance is at stake.

- DO consult your solicitor to ensure that, if you want to fire somebody, you obey the letter of the law and carry out the correct procedures.

- DO be prepared to carry out a major reorganisation of your practice every three to four years. If not, events will force change upon you when you don't want it.

- DON'T take the first assistant an employment agency sends you if they are not absolutely the kind you want. Talk to the agency and tell them what you did not like about the person they sent, and they will try to get nearer your job specification next time.

- DO use headhunters. They can often get top people, but remember once you let them into your confidence they keep their man on the mailing list for his next job.

- DON'T appoint senior people in your practice from outside until everyone knows you have tried to make the appointment from within.

- DON'T bring in relatives who have just qualified and put them into your hierarchy above more experienced and better qualified partners or staff. Let them go out and gain experience elsewhere. If you then want them, appoint them by consent as a valuable addition to the practice. After all, sometimes the offspring are better than the parents, but more often the reverse is true if the parent was the founder of the practice.

- DON'T be careless about appointing your receptionist/telephonist. They are the first contact with your organisation and you will want them to be friendly, intelligent, helpful, quick and sensitive, and look presentable too.

- DO phone your office and ask for yourself or one of your partners and see what happens.

- DO phone your office and ask yourself whether the response is efficient, friendly or downright rude.
- But DON'T be too assiduous in checking how the firm is working. DON'T keep pulling up the plants to see how the roots are growing.
- DON'T have a typing pool. Try to organise a secretarial service to the whole office with well trained and well paid secretaries who can serve everyone in the office when needed.
- DO keep your small practice in spartan condition. DON'T employ people from larger practices. They have become 'fat cats' used to supporting services which don't exist in the small practice.
- DON'T let the retiring partner become a consultant and have a room in your office. Persuade him to leave completely and do something else or only operate for the firm outside the office.
- DO make profit sharing related as directly as possible to individual performance.
- DON'T dilute bonuses — these should go to some members of the office and not others. The others will know how to get their rewards next year!
- DO let people in the office know how much everyone else earns, including the directors. Once they all know there are no more rumours. If they don't think they are properly rewarded, they can discuss it with their boss in an open comparative way and judgements are made on merit in full knowledge of the figures.
- DO keep your people under tight financial control. The best people excel in performance and find ways to meet tough budgets this way.
- DO let the staff see the annual accounts to see how the firm is doing. Secrecy makes for lost opportunities of staff help and involvement, and betrays trust.
- DON'T be too optimistic when planning time for production information. If you list the drawings needed and put time against each drawing and arrive at a total, double this figure and it should account for the immeasurable time spent getting information, checking consultants and sub-contractors' drawings and getting quotations.
- DO always plan peoples' time and engagement on projects rather than not plan any at all, even though the fluctuations in workloads and requirements of projects may make planning very difficult.

- DO measure the amount of time senior people spend at institute meetings. Willing people can get overloaded with nice, prestigious jobs which benefit institutes but not the practice (unless an OBE will get the next job).
- DON'T use 'flexi' hours. In our business we have to be available when everyone else is, including clients, builders, subcontractors and local authorities.
- DON'T have too many staff who are doing part-time day courses or studying: when you programme staff you normally allow for a four day week, taking into consideration holidays, sickness etc. All you get from staff on part time courses is three days a week, even though you may get more enthusiasm, keenness and perhaps extra development potential. But DO have some people of this type, and maintain links with the schools of architecture — this certainly benefits a practice.
- DON'T set up a branch office many miles from yours and expect to run it yourself. Both offices will suffer. Put a top person in charge of the new office and give them 100 per cent backing and delegation.
- DON'T employ a large management consultancy firm to solve your problems. If you want outside advice get an architect with a thorough management training and experience in the field to spend a few days in your office and report to all the partners or directors within seven days of the visit. Any more time leads to cover-ups and an over-complicated management report.
- DON'T install computers unless you also have someone in the office who has had at least two or three years' experience in using them. On average, most computers, whatever they are, take about nine months' learning time before their operation becomes cost effective. No computer has saved money. They just widen the service and give opportunities for greater information.
- DON'T buy graphic computers unless you are absolutely sure you have the resources to spend on an eighteen month learning curve. Graphic computers have never reduced architectural staff. They just improve your service facilities if properly used.

Further reading

ACCOUNTING AND FINANCIAL MANAGEMENT

Baggott, Joseph (1984) *Cost and Management Accounting Made Simple*

Barrow, Colin (1984) *Financial Management for the Small Business*

Bathurst, Peter E. and Butler, David A. (1980) *Building Cost Control: Techniques and Economics*

Grant, P. (1971) *Management and Financial Control in the Professional Office*

Murphy B. (1978) *Management Accounting* ('Teach Yourself' Series)

Pendlebury, M. (1984) *Company Accounts: A Guide*

Touche Ross & Co (1983) *Tolley's Survival Kit for Small Businesses: Financial Management in a Changing Economic Climate*

ARCHITECTURAL PRACTICE

Bennett, Philip H.P. (1981) *Architectural Practice and Procedure*

Bower, Jack (1978) *Small Works Contract Documentation and how to Administer It*

Cecil, Raymond (1984) *Professional Liability*

Moxely, R. (1984) *An Architect's Guide to Fee Negotiation*

Willis, A.J. and others (1981) *The Architect in Practice*

RIBA PUBLICATIONS

RIBA (1982) *Architect's Appointment: Main Works*

RIBA (1982) *Architect's Appointment: Small Works*
RIBA (1983) *Architect's Job Book*
RIBA (1984) *Clerk of Works Manual*
RIBA (1983) *Code of Professional Conduct*
RIBA (1980) *Handbook of Architectural Practice and Management*
RIBA (1985) *Indemnity and Insurance Aspects of Building Contracts*
RIBA (1983) *Job Costing* (cassette and booklet)
RIBA (1973) *Plan of Work for Design Team Operation*
RIBA (1976) *Resources Control*
RIBA (1982) *Schedule of Services and Fees: Main Works*
RIBA (1982) *Schedule of Services and Fees: Small Works*

COMPANIES AND PARTNERSHIPS

Coulson-Thomas, C.J. (1975) *Company Administration Made Simple*
Institute of Directors (1985) *Guidelines for Directors*
Moberly, William (1983) *Partnership Management*
Pitfield, R.R. (1983) *Company Practice Made Simple*
RIBA Salaried Architects Group (1982) *Architects' Co-operatives: An Introduction*
Roberts, Dennis (1983) *How to Form a Company*
RIBA (1965) *Group Practice and Consortia*
Williamson, S.L. (1983) *Selecting Small Business Systems*

FINANCING BUSINESS

Checkley, Keith (1984) *Finance for Small Business*
Institute of Directors (1982) *The Director's Guide to Sources of Finance for the Smaller Company*
Woodcock, Clive (1982) *Raising Finance: The Guardian Guide for the Small Business*

INFORMATION SOURCES AND SYSTEMS

Bradfield, Valerie J., editor (1983) *Information Sources in Architecture*

Donohue, Brian (1983) *How to Buy an Office Computer or Word Processor*

Horner, Howard (1984) *Computing in a Small Business*

Speaight, Anthony and Stone, Gregory (1985) *The AJ Legal Handbook*

Labour Relations Agency, Belfast (1981) *A Guide to Employment Law and Practice for the Small Organisation*

Newton, Steve (1984) *Graphics and Image in Office Systems*

MANAGEMENT

Breck, E.F.L. (1965) *Organisation: The Framework of Management*

Breck, E.F.L. (1983) *The Principles and Practice of Management*

Coxe, Weld (1980) *Managing Architectural and Engineering Practice*

Drucker, Peter F. (1977) *People and Performance*

Drucker, Peter F. (1955) *The Practice of Management*

McGregor, D. (1960) *The Human Side of Enterprise*

Open University Press (1983) *The Effective Manager* — Part 3: *You and your organisation*; Part 9: *Organisations*

RIBA (1962) *The Architect and his Office*

Sprott, W.H.J. (1958) *Human Groups*

Steward, W.C. and Day, G.J. (1978) *The Businessman's Complete Checklist*

Townsend, Robert (1971) *Up the Organisation*

Video Arts (1984) *The Unorganised Manager*

MARKETING

Coxe, Weld (1983) *Marketing Architectural and Engineering Services*

Golzen, Godfrey (1984) *How Architects Get Work*

Institute of Directors (1985) *Choosing and Using an Advertising Agency*

RIBA: London Media Group (1981) *An Architect's Guide to Marketing the Smaller Practice*

MISCELLANEOUS USEFUL BOOKS

Ferrier, Charles W. (1983) *Leasing and Hire*
Moroney, M.J. (1969) *Facts from Figures*
Chaplin, Paul R.G. (1983) *Choosing and Using Professional Advisers*
Coopers & Lybrand (1983) *Tax Saving for the Family Business*
Golzen, Godfrey (1984) *Working for Yourself*
The Guardian (1984) *Guide to Running a Small Business*
Prentis, Nigel (1983) *The Self Employment Fact Book*
ACAS (1985) *Employing People*

Index